Southern Seasons

*month - by - month gardening
in the Piedmont Plateau*

Written by
Frances Worthington

Illustrated by
Charles H. Shurcliff

D1478038

A publication of The Greenville News-Piedmont Co.
Greenville, S.C.

Dedication

For family, friends and fellow gardeners — past, present and future.

Credits:

Cover and inside illustrations by Charles H. Shurcliff
Cover design by Kevin Walker
Back cover map design by Suzie Riddle
Back cover photograph by Fred Rollison
Edited by Ann L. Clark

ISBN: 0-9620923-1-2 10.95

Preface

Denizens of planet Earth who live in the mid-south region of North America geologically designated as the Piedmont Plateau know full well it has one of the most agreeable climates in the galaxy. The moderate weather allows us to do outdoor work on a year-round basis yet the temperature swings are wide enough to create dramatic seasonal changes as our blue and green globe revolves around the sun.

Wonderful as it is, this climate can also be a very demanding one for avid gardeners. We must do the right thing at absolutely the right time. Forget to cut back the monkey grass early enough, for instance, and the old leaves will be a tattered mess for the next ten months. Plant cool-weather things too late and they will languish in the rising heat of late spring. Ignore a rampant wisteria vine for more than a few minutes and it may smother a favorite tree or tear the gutters from the house. The list goes on and on.

After spending more than a decade coping with my own Piedmont Plateau garden, I have finally settled on the schedule detailed in this book. It is based on personal experience plus the knowledgeable advice of other gardeners in this area, including friends, neighbors, nurserymen, fellow writers, extension agents, landscape designers and intrepid readers of my newspaper column who have taken the time to call or write.

Please use the monthly reminders as a general outline and not as a mandate. The mini-climate of each garden is as unique as the gardener who tends it. Rural gardeners and those along the northern border of the Piedmont Plateau will probably find themselves waiting a few extra days for the last frost while urban dwellers and gardeners who reside near the southern border can set out marigolds and tomatoes earlier but may have to hold back a little on sowing fall lettuce.

Fine-tune the schedule to suit your particular garden by writing in extra reminders, observations and even disagreements. If your notes are legible, the book should become an increasingly valuable guide to nurturing healthy, beautiful, productive plants.

On the other hand, should the advice prove to be of little help, or should your handwriting be indecipherable, please feel free to indulge yourself in that act of organic catharsis that has consoled frustrated gardeners for several centuries: Take this book and compost it!

Good luck and best wishes for happy gardening in all the months to come.

— Frances Worthington

January

January nights often drop below freezing, although some days are very mild, and there may be snow or ice storms. Main tasks include caring for house plants, ordering plants and seeds from catalogs, planning the spring garden and collecting potting soil and containers in which to start flower and vegetable transplants.

On mild days outdoor work may include watering, liming and even some planting.

In dry winters, it is especially important to remember to water perennials, fruit plants, evergreens and newly planted trees or shrubs.

If weather is warm, the end of January is a good time to

clean up leaves, weeds and overlooked dead annuals. It is not wise to leave the ground bare under shrubs or in perennial beds, so apply new mulch after raking off any old leaves. Use purchased materials or simply shred the leaves and spread them back in place. Shredded leaves won't blow away as easily as whole leaves so the yard will stay neater.

Tools should be cleaned and checked once a year. January is a good time to do it. Clean and protect metal implements like shovels by moving the blade up and down in a bucket of coarse sand over which a quart of salad oil has been poured.

Paint handles a bright color so they can be seen easily or rub linseed oil into bare wood to help preserve it. File edges of hoes and shovels, sharpen clippers and have lawnmowers, shredders and other gas-powered machines serviced as necessary.

Plant protection

In January, it's important to protect certain plants from winter damage. Shake or brush snow off evergreen plants to minimize limb breakage. Ice cannot safely be removed, but smaller plants can be protected before storms begin by covering them with burlap, a cardboard box or a fabric-covered cage of wire fencing or wood strips.

Lime and wood ashes

Spread agricultural (dolomitic) lime on lawn, vegetable garden and flower plots, according to results from soil tests made last fall. Apply with spreader or, in small areas, with a flour sifter or even by hand. Do not apply lime to centipede lawns or other acid-loving plants like blueberries, wildflowers, camellias, azaleas and rhododendrons unless a soil test indicates the need for it.

Wood ashes from your fireplace or wood stove also contain calcium and are a good source of many other trace elements; substitute them for lime on a one-to-one basis by weight. Fresh coal ashes can be detrimental to plants, so avoid their use.

If no tests were done but you suspect some lime is needed on the lawn or in the vegetable garden, a fairly safe rate of annual lime or wood ash application is one pound per 100 square feet of soil surface. This translates into approximately one to one-and-a-half measuring cups of lime or one to three cups of wood ashes (ashes are often very fluffy and thus weigh less than an equal volume of lime).

Compost, other organic material

Most Southern soils contain only 1 percent organic matter, yet the ideal for great gardening, especially great organic gardening, is to maintain a level of 5 percent. This requires the yearly application of as much as 200 pounds of organic matter per 100 square feet of soil each year — no small task!

As an absolute minimum, spread a half-inch of organic matter over vegetable and flower plots each year and work it lightly into the top few inches of soil.

Add shredded leaves, aged sawdust or partially rotted manure sometime between mid-October and the end of January. If you use finished compost (homemade or purchased), wait until shortly before planting to add it to the soil.

Lawns

Thin fescue or bluegrass lawns should be dressed with processed manure, finished compost or one of the organic fertilizers now on the market.

If wild onions and garlic are a problem, January is a good time to deal with them. Although various chemical treatments can be employed, hand-weeding of these bulbous plants is easier on the environment and often more effective than herbicides. When ground is moist enough to allow easy penetration, slide a knife or other thin blade into the soil next to a plant — or next to a clump of several plants — and wiggle it to loosen roots. Pull plant leaves gently upward so the bulbs are brought out of the ground. Any bulbs left behind will sprout again next year.

Ground covers, ornamental grasses

Wait until next month to cut back liriope and mondo unless you're just in the mood to get it over with. Grasses like pampas, miscanthus and rose fountain can be cut back whenever they begin to be unsightly.

Shrubs and trees

Both container-grown and bare-rooted shrubs and trees can be planted or transplanted this month whenever the ground isn't frozen. Mulch new plantings and keep them watered. Spray newly planted evergreens, including live Christmas trees, with an anti-transpirant.

Roses

Roses like to grow in soil that has a nearly neutral pH, something that can be difficult to maintain in naturally acidic soil or in gardens where acid rain falls. A good way to meet their needs is to apply a half-cup of pelletized or pulverized lime to the soil around each bush twice a year, once now and again in June.

Bamboos

These large members of the grass family can be transplanted anytime between now and the end of February to start a grove in a new location. The easiest approach is to dig up some of the horizontal roots and trim off all of the above-ground stalks. Cut the roots into sections that are two to four feet long. Plant them just a couple of inches deep in moderately rich soil, spreading them out horizontally as they grew before. New shoots should appear in April.

To move smaller varieties, dig up a clump that has several stalks, plus a good-sized ball of soil, and move the whole thing to a new place.

In either case, lime the soil after planting and then fertilize as soon as new growth appears. Keep well-watered for the first year since even a short drought can be deadly.

Spring bulbs

Although spring bulbs won't open their flowers until next month, many bulbs will send up exploratory leaves if the weather is warm. Should this happen, don't worry. They'll still bloom at the appointed time. Some gardeners like to rake off all fallen leaves from bulb areas at this time, leaving the ground bare. Others rake them off, then shred and replace them to make a light mulch which won't interfere with the bloom spikes as they emerge. Do whichever pleases you best.

Early January is a good time to fertilize many spring bulbs, especially crocuses and daffodils, if you did not feed them in November or December. Tulips are the exception to this rule and should be fed only in the fall if you hope to keep them going for more than a year.

Forced bulbs

Continue watering pots of spring bulbs that are being forced into early bloom and fertilize as you did last month with one teaspoon of bulb granules per pot or with a high-phosphorus liquid houseplant food. Bulbs that have been in a cool place for ten to fifteen weeks may begin to show signs of growth. When two inches of leaf show above ground and you can also see the flower buds, plants are ready to be moved into a frost-free location in bright but indirect light. As the leaves turn green and begin to grow, place in a sunny window; flowers should spring up shortly. Bring only one or two pots of bulbs out each week so that you will have a steady stream of new blossoms.

As blooms fade, the easiest thing to do is to discard the plants to the compost heap. Should you decide to try to bring them to maturity for use in the garden next year, put them in a sunny place and water regularly.

Geraniums and wax begonias

Take geranium and wax begonia cuttings from plants that have been growing in a windowsill. They'll be big enough to transplant in April. Or be bold and try starting some from seed under lights.

Annual flowers

Outdoors, plant seeds of hardy annuals. Sprinkle small seeds, like poppies and alyssum, on the surface of roughly raked earth in late January or early February but do not cover. The seeds will gradually drop into crevices on their own and sprout in early spring. Plant larger seeds, like larkspur and cornflower, in furrows according to package directions.

Indoor seedlings: January 20-30, start slow-growing annuals, including alyssum, coleus, datura, lobelia, mimulus, geranium, vinca and heliotrope. Pansies can be started from seed now, put outside in March and they will bloom through June and sometimes continue into early July.

Perennial flowers

This is the time to start any perennials that you wish to grow from seed. Pay careful attention to packet instructions; some seeds require special temperatures or treatments to induce sprouting.

Herbs

Plant chive seeds to transplant outdoors in March or April.

Vegetables

Fall and winter crops, like collards, kale, radishes, turnips, mustard greens and leeks can still be harvested in many gardens, as can lettuce that has been grown under a cloche or row covering. Fall-planted onions and spinach may have been killed back by freezes, but they will resprout and continue to grow in February or March.

Water vegetables during dry spells but fertilize only those that seem to be actively growing. Mulch carrots, radishes and turnips to keep the tops of the roots from freezing; pull and eat them any time.

Onion plants and cabbage transplants begin to be available at some Piedmont feed'n'seed stores late in the month. They can be planted outside but run the risk of being killed back if no extra protection is provided.

Toward the end of the month, weed the asparagus bed. Broadcast about two pounds (4 cups) of fertilizer granules, organic or synthetic, per 100 square feet. Renew the mulch after feeding.

During the first half of the month turn under cover crops in the garden. Mow the tall ones first to make handling easier.

Indoor seedlings: Jan. 1-15, start cabbage, celery and lettuce (leaf and head), Jan. 16-30, make second plantings of cabbage and lettuce. Start broccoli during the last week.

Orchard and fruit

Weed and feed established beds of strawberries at the end of the month. If mulch has thinned, put down additional straw or pine needles. Some fruit trees, including apples, peaches and pears, appreciate an annual application of lime, which may be done now.

House plants

Remove dead leaves and flowers; snip off lanky growth. Add a handful or two of fresh potting mix to the top of the containers whose soil has settled too low.

Clean fuzzy-leafed plants by brushing lightly with a soft paintbrush. Give small, smooth-leaved plants a bath by washing them with tepid water in the shower or kitchen sink. Clean dusty leaves of large plants by wiping with a wet cloth. Do not use commercial leaf shine products that may clog plant pores.

Plants that were dormant in December may start growing again in late January. If so, resume regular fertilization. You may want to apply a spoonful of guano or water plants with fish emulsion at this time since these contain all sorts of necessary trace elements that chemical house plant fertilizers lack.

Check plants carefully for insects, especially mealy bugs and spider mites. Mealy bugs look like tiny pieces of cotton fluff.

Wipe them off with a wet cloth or with an ear swab that has been dipped in rubbing alcohol.

Spider mites like dry conditions and thus are often prevalent in the winter when forced-air heating removes moisture from household air. They look like tiny red or gray, eight-legged dots and as the numbers rise, they may spin messy webs to hold eggs and molting adults. These insects are very hard to see, so use a magnifying glass to inspect the undersides of leaves. Banish mites by giving plants a bath in tepid water; follow this with a spray of insectical soap (like Safer's), being sure to hit the underside of each leaf. Mist plants daily with water and repeat soapy spray after two weeks if new mites are seen.

Notes

Notes

February

February can feel like spring one day and winter the next as snow or icy rains buffet tender plants. Hard freezes are a regular occurrence but early crocuses and daffodils manage to open their blooms anyway. There is usually enough precipitation to preclude the need for extra watering, but root rot can be a danger in soggy ground. Check low-lying spots for standing water and dig drainage trenches as necessary.

Re-read January tasks for information on plant protection, planting of trees and shrubs, and applications of lime, wood ashes and organic matter. Be sure to finish tasks left undone from last month.

Weeds

Hardy invaders like henbit, dock and chickweed are prevalent during late winter. February is a good time to pull or hoe them out, before they set seed and scatter everywhere.

Dormant oil spray

Dormant oil spray is an effective way to control scale and other sucking insects like aphids, mealybugs, spider mites and thrips. The mist of oil coats and suffocates overwintering insects and/or their eggs without harming birds or animals. Mix according to label directions and use on deciduous shrubs, fruit trees, flowering cherry and peach trees and on evergreen ornamental shrubs like camellias and gardenias. Spray only on a non-windy, warm day when the temperature is above 40°F and no rain is expected. Cover backs of leaves as well as fronts.

Lawns

Feed fescue and other cool weather grasses at mid-month with a slow-release formula. Areas plagued by crabgrass last year can be treated with a pre-emergent crabgrass preventer during the last week of the month. Wait until March if there is snow on the ground.

Buy plain crabgrass preventer for warm-season grasses or a formula that includes lawn fertilizer for bluegrass and fescue. Spread at rate recommended on package. Crabgrass seedlings will be killed as they try to sprout in late March, leaving plenty of room for more desirable grasses to fill in. Note that crabgrass preventer will stop regular grass seed from sprouting and cannot be used when reseeding bare areas.

Ground covers, ornamental grasses

Liriope, most ferns and perennial grasses like miscanthus, rose fountain and pampas should receive an annual haircut in February, before new growth begins. Cut liriope back to within an inch of ground level using clippers, a string trimmer or even a mower if the earth is level. Mondo grass doesn't have to be trimmed annually, so cut it only if the leaves have become ragged or yellowed.

Cut shorter grasses back to three inches and tall ones to about a foot. Use tough pruning shears on the sharp-edged grasses and wear gloves to protect your hands.

Overgrown clumps of liriope, mondo and ornamental grasses, including pampas, can be dug up, divided into several sections and replanted. Or they can simply be moved to a new place if relocation is the aim.

Indoor seedlings: Start seeds of annual ornamental grasses like panic grass and animated oats this month. Many seeds will take three or four weeks to germinate, but most will be ready for the garden by late April.

Trees

Fertilize trees toward the end of the month. Apply one cup of 5-10-10 (or organic equivalent) per inch of trunk diameter. Scratch fertilizer into soil under canopy of smaller trees and water. For larger trees, punch ten more holes in the soil near the drip-line and pour fertilizer in. A simpler but more expensive method is to drive fertilizer tree spikes into ground at recommended rate.

Pruning

Although many plants can be pruned at other times of the year, February is a good choice since the general load of gardening chores is light and the lack of leaves on deciduous plants makes it easier to decide what to do. If weather is freezing at the start of the month, wait until it moderates during the last couple of weeks.

In general, remove only those limbs that are diseased, damaged or dead, rub together, or grow inward and block light. You may also want to remove lower branches to show off the interesting bark on the trunks of trees like crape myrtle and river birch.

Cut suckers from the bases of trees or single-trunked shrubs. Also remove water sprouts (the unattractively vertical shoots that spring up wildly from many of the horizontal branches of dogwoods, crabapples and other small trees).

Take off thick limbs by first sawing upwards for a half-inch through the underside of the limb; then cut downwards from above. This pattern of cuts will allow the limb to break cleanly, without ripping off the extra bark.

Although it is traditional to paint large pruning wounds with a fungicidal compound, recent studies have shown this to be unnecessary. If you feel the need to do something anyway, cover the cuts with leftover latex house paint which is light in color.

Lightly prune ornamental evergreens like gardenias, andromedas, rhododendrons and camellias. Remove just a branch or two here and there to allow the natural shape to show through. Shrubs that continually throw up new canes, like nandina, forsythia and quince, should be pruned by cutting off a third of the old canes at ground level each year.

Although some gardeners like to wait until after the blooming period to prune shrubs that will flower before June 1 (like azalea, forsythia, quince and mockorange), it is fine to prune them now if you don't mind sacrificing some flowers.

The amount of buddleia pruning to do is a very personal choice about which avid gardeners can argue for hours. Some people cut them back every year at this time to a foot in height, believing that this scalping results in a better shape and more flowers during the summer. Others trim more moderately, hoping for taller specimens. If the winter is severe, the whole question will be moot since the buddleias will be killed back to the ground and everything dead will have to be trimmed off as the new growth emerges in the spring. So do as the spirit moves you and hope for the best.

Revitalize hopelessly overgrown shrubs like hollies, privet, flowering quince and even some azaleas by cutting them back all the way, to within just a foot of the ground. They'll resprout and grow quickly when warm weather arrives.

Needle-leaved evergreens like yew and juniper must be treated carefully because they grow slowly and do not recover easily from excessive cuts. Prune lightly if at all, just enough to neaten the natural appearance. Do not cut a limb back beyond the set of needle-bearing side branches closest to the trunk; if pruned further, the whole branch usually dies rather than sprouting new growth.

Do not prune common blue and pink hydrangeas until later in the spring when you can be sure what's dead and what isn't.

Hedges

General trimming can be done now but the hedge may look unattractive afterward; it's better to wait until mid-March or early April when new leaves will quickly grow to cover the pruning scars.

Vines

Prune silver fleece vine severely because it flowers on new wood. Plant sweet peas during the last half of the month.

Indoor seedlings: February 5-20, start seeds of annual vines that need eight to ten weeks of growth to reach transplant size, including cypress and moonflower vines.

February 20-28, start seeds of nasturtium vines in peat pots so you'll be able to plant pot and all to avoid too much root disturbance, something nasturtium hates.

Roses

New plants are usually available at local nurseries toward the end of the month and can be planted anytime.

Established roses should be pruned back in late February or early March, depending on the weather and on how soon the roses begin putting on new growth. The rarely realized goal is to prune early in mild winters, late in severe ones. Find out which type of rose you have (shrub, hybrid tea, climber, etc.) because each requires a slightly different treatment.

In general, cut out dead, diseased or weak wood and then cut back healthy canes by one-third to a half, making the cut just above an outward-facing bud. Don't prune spring-flowering climbers until later, after they have finished flowering.

Remove and dispose of all pruned material. If you keep a mulch on the plants, consider raking up the old stuff and replacing it with new material to help get rid of the disease spores and overwintering insects that can affect plants during the growing season.

Roses often benefit from a thorough spraying of lime sulfur in early February before any spring growth starts. It helps control many troublesome rose diseases, including canker, powdery mildew and blackspot. Apply spray after pruning and putting down the new mulch, being sure to wet both the bushes and the mulch or soil underneath.

Spring and summer bulbs

Anemone and ranunculus bulbs can be planted this month. Lily bulbs can also be bought and planted if they are available.

Forced bulbs

Continue with the same treatment mentioned in January's notes.

Geraniums and wax begonias

Cuttings that were taken last month can be potted up in small individual containers as soon as roots are well-established.

Annual and perennial flowers

Continue planting seeds of hardy annuals outdoors during the first half of the month.

Indoor seedlings: February 5-20, start seeds of flowers that need eight to ten weeks of growth to reach transplant size, including ageratum, arctotis, brownwallia, China aster, dahlias like Piccolo and Rigoletto, dusty miller, flowering maple, annual foxglove, gerbera daisy, hibiscus, hollyhock, penstemon, petunia, snapdragons, and Tohoku daisy.

Herbs

Set out horseradish roots whenever the weather allows.

Indoor seedlings: February 1-15, start parsley seeds. Also sow chives if you didn't in January. February 16-28, start seeds of basil, borage, coriander, dill, summer savory and sweet marjoram.

Vegetables

February is the real beginning of spring for avid vegetable gardeners because many transplants are started indoors and a few things can actually be planted outside.

Fertilize established asparagus beds if not done last month and check weekly for signs of sprouts. Begin harvesting as soon as the first ones are six to eight inches tall and continue the harvest for six weeks. New crowns can be planted throughout the month.

Set out transplants of cabbage, head lettuce and leaf lettuce, preferably under the protection of a cloche or floating row cover. These early plants may occasionally be killed back by exceptionally low temperatures, but most years they will survive and yield well.

February 1-15, plant seeds of head and leaf lettuce, endive, mustard, rape and radish. Cover newly seeded areas with a row cover to induce faster, more even germination.

February 16-28, make a second planting of head and leaf lettuce, mustard, rape and radish. Also sow seeds of spinach and turnips. Put out onion sets or plants.

Plant seeds of English, Snow and Sugar Snap peas, covering them with a half-inch of soil. For faster germination, soak seeds for a couple of hours in tepid water. Peas sprout best when soil temperature is above 50°F. If earth is too cool, cover plantings with clear plastic or an agricultural row covering to trap heat. Unless seeds have been treated with a fungicide, dust them with a legume inoculant before planting.

Indoor seedlings: February 1-15, start seeds of broccoli, cabbage, leaf and head lettuce. February 16-28, start seeds of cabbage, cauliflower and a last round of leaf lettuce. Try a heat-resistant variety since it will mature during warm weather. For super-large tomato transplants, start seeds now but be prepared to re-pot in bigger containers after a few weeks.

Orchard and fruit

It's time to prune fruit trees, bushes and vines of all sorts, including hardy kiwi, bunch grapes and muscadines. Apply dormant oil to fruit trees as described above.

At the end of the month feed fruit trees, nuts, grapes and kiwis with a complete fertilizer, taking into account the age of each plant and following directions on container. Pecan trees often need extra zinc, so you may want to buy a fertilizer that has been amended with this mineral. Fertilize fig trees by mulching with bagged manure or finished compost.

Indoors, start alpine and other from-seed strawberries during the first half of the month. Outdoors, you can set out virtually any new plant, whether it be tree, bush, bramble or vine.

Strawberry plants can be planted in late February or early March. In established strawberry beds, separate and transplant extra baby plants to a new area.

Fertilize blueberry bushes with cottonseed meal or other acid organic fertilizer and then mulch with pine needles or shredded oak leaves.

House plants

Indoor plants become more vigorous as spring approaches, so the last half of February is a good time to prune the overgrown ones and repot those that are too large for the container. For best results, use a good quality potting mix which contains vermiculite and trace minerals as well as peat. Loosen roots and shake off some of the old soil before transferring to the new pot.

Prune allamanda to keep it husky and cut back new shoots to within two or three swollen nodes of old wood. Repot after pruning if necessary and then begin fertilizing twice a month to push it toward lush blooms in late March or early April. Do the same for mandevillea if you are overwintering vines that were used outdoors last summer.

Divide and repot house plants that have formed new crowns or offsets, like the African violet, various bromeliads, cape primrose (Streptocarpus), snake plant (Sanseveria), pregnant onion, ivy, asparagus fern, and Boston or Dallas fern. Snip and root babies from spider plants, piggy-back plants and strawberry begonias.

This is also a good time to take cuttings from many indoor plants, including philodendron, pepperomia, rex begonia, scented geranium, jade tree and devil's ivy.

Notes

March

Some March days are quite warm, but night frosts are frequent, a hard freeze may hit any time and high winds often cause damage to shrubs and trees. Many perennials begin to show new growth this month and a number of eager plants may open their flowers, especially if it has been a mild winter. Keep an eye out for candytuft, hyacinths, grape hyacinths, daffodils, violets, Star of Bethlehem, early tulips, spirea, forsythia, Japanese magnolia, flowering plum, weeping cherry and redbud.

March is a very busy time for gardeners who start seedlings indoors because so many flowers and vegetables must be sown now to be ready for transplant in April.

Lawns

Warm-season grasses that were overplanted with rye should be mowed very closely. De-thatch Bermuda, centipede and zoysia lawns if necessary to get them ready for new growth in April.

Cool-weather grasses, like fescue, really begin to grow again. Feed immediately if no fertilizer was applied in February.

Apply crabgrass preventer during the first week of March if not done last month. If crabgrass preventer mixed with fertilizer was applied in late February, don't feed again this month.

March is a good time to sow seeds of cool-season grasses, whether it's to start a new lawn or re-seed bare patches. For best results, buy a turf fescue hybridized for your particular area and avoid mixes that contain lots of annual rye since the rye will die off in just a few months. If you are starting a new lawn, consider experimenting with one of the dwarf fescues now on the market. In the months and years to come, they will need far less mowing than the taller varieties.

Scratch grass seed and seedling fertilizer into well-tilled and raked ground. Mulch lightly with straw or floating row cover. Sprinkle daily until grass germinates, then water once or twice a week during dry spells. Do remember that seeding won't work in areas that have been recently treated with pre-emergent crabgrass killer.

Ground covers, ornamental grasses

Liriope should begin to put up new leaves this month. Make sure the old ones have been clipped back beforehand.

Liriope and trailing vinca need little fertilization unless soil is very poor. Mondo grass, ajuga, lamb's ears, pachysandra and most other ground covers will appreciate a top-dressing of finished compost, a light dose of slow-release lawn fertilizer or a dose of organic granules. Also feed hosta when the first leaves begin to poke up.

Most perennial ornamental grasses won't show new growth until April. Cut them back now if not done last month. Late in the month, look for seedlings of annual grasses grown last year and either weed them out or transplant to a new location.

Hedges

If hedges are pruned in March, new leaves will soon come out to cover the scars. Aim for a pyramidal shape, wider at the bottom than at the top and feed after pruning.

Shrubs

Most shrubs should be given a maintenance application of fertilizer at the end of the month, including those planted during the past fall or winter. Use a balanced, slow-release fertilizer to ensure that nitrogen is not released too quickly. Apply four ounces (about ½ cup) of granular fertilizer per 10 square feet of ground or follow directions on the package. Scratch fertilizer into earth around plants, placing it under any existing mulches and water thoroughly after application.

Many common azaleas can be fed now, though some hybrids may show flower damage from early fertilization. To be safe, wait until later in the spring, after blossoms have faded.

Camellias that have been damaged by cold weather may drop their flower buds, but this will not affect next year's performance. Feed fall-blooming camellias now. Feed winter and spring camellias as soon as flowering finishes., which may not be until early next month. Just before feeding, clean off old mulch and dispose of any fallen flowers to forestall disease problems. Scratch fertilizer into soil, water, and then put on new mulch.

Inspect big-leaf hydrangeas (often called French hydrangeas) toward the end of March. Cut off any dead stems at ground level. If shrub is too tall, prune remaining stems back by ½ to ¾, cutting off just above a live bud which is swelling and/or beginning to show some green.

Fertilize hydrangeas along with other shrubs. For those that respond to soil pH by shifting the color of their blooms, use an acidic fertilizer to produce blue blooms. Liming the soil will encourage pink blossoms, but in soils that are neutral, both pink and blue blooms may be present, as well as lavender ones.

Peegee hydrangeas are more attractive if trained into a small tree with strong, arching stems. To achieve this, prune the lowest branches each spring and trim out any especially weak growth. After a few years of this routine, none of the flowers will drag on the ground, no matter how heavy they are.

Vines

Fertilize most perennial vines toward the end of the month, including akebia, trumpet honeysuckle, porcelain, ivy, climbing hydrangea, crossvine and Dutchman's pipe. Mulch clematis vines with about two inches of finished compost and apply a cup of pelletized or pulverized lime. Feed new trumpet creeper (Campsis) with a layer of compost plus two tablespoonfuls of bone meal; older vines rarely need extra feedings.

Prune vines that will bloom in summer, like bittersweet, climbing hydrangea, bignonia, trumpet creeper and porcelain vine. Cut back extra growth and remove dead parts. Prune silver fleece if not done last month. Also cut back English and Boston ivy.

To prune a clematis vine correctly, you need to know what type it is and when it flowers. Most spring-flowering types bloom on last season's wood, so don't prune these much at all except to remove dead, diseased or injured parts. Those that flower later in the year on the current season's growth, including Jackman, Lord Neville, Ernest Markham and the rampant sweet autumn clematis, can be cut back as necessary to keep them in place; they will still give you plenty of blossoms.

Indoor seedlings: March 1-15, sow seeds of most annual vines, including cup-and-saucer, black-eyed Susan and morning glory.

Roses

Give rose bushes a first feeding in mid-to-late March as new growth begins to leaf out. Use a commercial slow-release rose fertilizer or organic granules. Or apply a mulch of freshly finished compost and then water with manure tea, fish emulsion or liquid kelp.

Begin a regular spray or dusting routine for roses that are susceptible to diseases or that were greatly troubled by insects the previous year. Remember that not all roses require this maintenance; many shrub and "old" roses are naturally resistant to most diseases and pests. If you must spray, read labels first and look for the least environmentally lethal ingredients.

Spring bulbs

No care of spring bulbs is required except the snipping off of fading flowers so seed pods won't form and drain energy from the bulb that is trying to store up food for next year.

Lily bulbs can be purchased and planted as they become available.

Forced bulbs

If you saved the spring-flowering bulbs that were forced to bloom indoors, like hyacinths, daffodils and crocuses, plant them in the yard now. Keep the soil ball intact, settle gently into place and allow the foliage to continue to mature on its own. If you're lucky, the bulbs will bloom again next year.

Paperwhite narcissus bulbs that have bloomed should probably be discarded since they are not likely to rebloom when kept indoors until next year. In the warmest areas, try planting them outdoors in a protected place. If they survive, they will flower in December or January.

Summer bulbs and tubers

Caladium, dahlia and tuberous begonia tubers can be purchased or unearthed from winter storage. Plant indoors in deep flats or pots; after they sprout, grow them in a sunny window or under lights until they can be set outdoors in late April (or mid-May for the heat-loving caladium).

Geraniums

Plants that were stored in the basement during the winter should be brought out and rejuvenated at the start of the month. Prune, repot in new soil, soak thoroughly with lukewarm water, drain and put in a warm place. As growth begins, move into a sunny window and begin regular watering and fertilizing.

Continue caring for cuttings that were taken in January and potted last month.

Geraniums that were kept growing in a windowsill all winter, and which you plan to put outdoors in the summer, should be trimmed back now to induce stockier growth. This includes the scented varieties.

Perennial flowers

Healthy transplants are available at many local nurseries or will be arriving in the mail from previous catalog orders. They can be planted any time, along with any perennial seedlings you have grown at home.

Prepare ground for planting by stripping off grass, tilling or digging at least a foot deep and adding necessary amendments to poor soil (limestone, peat moss, sand, processed manure, etc.) Work in a low-nitrogen fertilizer, a chemical 5-10-10, an organic 5-3-4 or something similar, (using six to eight cups per 100 square feet).

If possible, water soil thoroughly and let settle for a few days. Then tamp soil down before planting to minimize later settling of newly turned earth.

A light sprinkling of bone meal and lime plus some low-nitrogen fertilizer will benefit most beds of established perennials. Use a 5-10-10 formula (a half-cup per square yard of ground), an organic mix recommended for ornamentals or an inch-deep layer of finished compost.

Established perennials that bloom in summer or fall can be dug up, divided and replanted in late March or early April if they've become too crowded. These include daylily, coreopsis, perennial phlox, purple coneflower, bee balm, gaillardia, gerbera daisy and goldenrod. Don't divide spring-blooming perennials now since it may interfere with flowering. See April notes for chrysanthemum and mealycup sage.

Look around for self-sown seedlings of perennials and half-hardy annuals like purple coneflower, larkspur, lenten rose, columbine, althea zebrina and money plant. Thin to appropriate spacing or dig up extras and move to a new home.

Dig and divide crowded hosta plants when new leaves begin to pop up in late March or early April. Handle with caution because the new growth is extremely brittle. Actually, it's much easier to divide them in the fall just as the old leaves are dying back, so wait if you can.

Annual flowers

Feed pansies and cut off fading flowers to encourage continued blooming. Pull up and compost ornamental kale and cabbage as they begin to bolt and become unattractive.

Many annuals will be offered for sale during the last half of March. Although few hardy ones, like pansies, snapdragons and alyssum, can be set out immediately, most annuals are tender and cannot go out until after the last frost. So, hold off as long as possible on the buying, even if the weather is lovely!

Do not plant annual seeds outside except for hardy ones that actually like to sprout in cool weather, like annual candytuft, alyssum, annual coreopsis, sweet William, California poppies, sweet peas and Virginia stock.

Continue to feed and water seedlings planted in February. Transplant to larger containers as necessary.

Indoor seedlings, March 1-15, start seeds of most summer annuals, including cleome, cosmos, blue lace flower, gaillardia, marigold, strawflower, balsam, burning bush, four-o'clock, nicotiana and portulaca. March 16-30, start seeds of the heat-loving annuals that do not like to be transplanted outside until nights stay above 50°F, including cockscomb, gazania, African daisy and zinnia.

Herbs

Transplants of hardy herbs, including chives, thyme and rosemary, are usually available for purchase and can be set out now. Plant parsley seeds outdoors or set out transplants. Hold off until mid-to-late April, a week or two after the final frost, before setting out tender herbs like basil and sesame. Trim thyme plants back by at least a third so that new growth will be forced from the center of the plant.

Indoor seedlings: March 1-15, start seeds of cilentro and basil.

Vegetables

Transplants of many hardy vegetables are available at feed'n'seed stores and nurseries (or are already growing under your own lights).

Set out tubers of Jerusalem artichokes any time. Put them in a separate bed where they cannot easily spread into surrounding areas and take over.

Harvest overwintered kale before it bolts. Feed overwintered lettuce and spinach to encourage rapid growth of tender leaves. Continue harvesting asparagus spears from established beds.

Radishes not picked in the fall will bloom in April and produce edible seed pods. If you'd like to experiment with this crop, pick two or three strong plants that show no sign of rot. Weed the area where they are growing and then apply a light sprinkling of fertilizer.

Buy seed potatoes (white, not sweet potatoes!) in mid-March and cut into planting pieces. Each piece should be the size of a chicken egg and should contain at least two eyes. Spread pieces out on newspaper in a corner of the house and allow them to dry for several days so the cut surfaces can form a protective callus. Plant outdoors during the last half of the month.

March 1-15, set out asparagus crowns, onion plants or sets, shallot sets and transplants of broccoli, cabbage, cauliflower, collards, leeks, leaf lettuce and head lettuce. Plant seeds of hardy vegetables, including beets, carrots, kohlrabi, Hon Tsai Tai, leaf and head lettuce, mustard, radishes, rape, spinach, santoh and turnips.

March 16-31, continue to set out asparagus crowns, broccoli, cabbage, collards, onions and shallots. Set out celery under a cloche or other protective covering. Plant potato sets. Make a first sowing of Swiss chard, comfrey, watercress and asparagus peas. Make additional plantings of beets, carrots, kohlrabi, leaf lettuce and turnips. In mild years try an early planting of corn; cover newly seeded area with floating row cover or plastic until after the last frost.

Indoor seedlings: March 1-15, start Malabar or New Zealand spinach, Swiss chard and tomato. Start sweet potato slips by placing an unsprayed tuber lengthwise in a container of moist potting soil. Set in a warm, sunny place and several sprouts will gradually emerge. When the sprouts have several leaves and have formed roots, they can be gently pulled free from the main tuber (more sprouts will emerge). Plant them outside right away if it's warm enough or inside in small pots until time for transplanting in mid-May. March 16-30, start seeds of cantaloupe, corn, cucumbers, eggplant, gourds, pepper, summer squash and watermelon.

Orchard and fruit

Continue to buy and set out blueberry bushes, strawberry plants and bramble fruits. Fertilize the strawberries as they are set into the ground. During the last half of the month set out container-grown figs and pomegranates.

Feed bramble fruits now. Also feed fruit trees, blueberries, nuts, kiwis and grapes if not done in February.

It is sometimes difficult to raise tree fruits completely organically. Many gardeners choose to apply two or three chemical sprays at the start of the season when insects are trying to lay eggs in the young fruits, then they leave the trees unsprayed for the rest of the summer. Some experimentation will be necessary to determine the best routine for your own garden, but the first spray is generally done at the time of bud swell, which occurs this month on many fruit trees. Don't spray when flowers are open and being pollinated because you don't want to kill the honeybees. The only exception to this rule is spraying done to control fire blight.

Plum, cherry and apricot trees bloom during March in most areas of the Piedmont Plateau. Late frosts will kill blossoms on these trees every few years, but that won't affect the next year's fruit production.

Blueberries can also bloom early and thus be harmed by a severe frost, reducing or even destroying the year's berry production. Watch plants and listen to weather forecasts. Be prepared to protect bushes with row covering, sheets or burlap.

House plants

As roots develop on cuttings you took in February, gently move each baby plant to a pot of its own.

House plants shouldn't be set outdoors permanently, no matter how mild the air may seem, though they can certainly be put out in a warm rain for a leaf wash. With longer days, most of our indoor guests begin growing vigorously and need regular fertilization.

Give mandevilla vines a high phosphorous fertilizer like a 10-

20-10 to encourage it to begin forming flower buds before it is placed outdoors for the summer. Not all water-soluble fertilizers contain trace elements like iron, copper and zinc, so read labels. Fertilize occasionally with a food that does have these trace elements, perhaps guano, fish emulsion, liquid kelp or a complete synthetic.

Cineria seeds planted indoors this month, kept outside in pots over the summer and then brought inside before frost should bloom next winter.

Notes

Notes

April

An April fool is a gardener who plants warm-weather annuals and vegetables too soon. Misled by a string of warm days, she/he marches out to the garden in early April, proudly puts in tomatoes, zinnias, marigolds and cucumbers ... then watches in dismay as a last cold snap decimates the plantings.

The last freeze may be as early as the first of April in some parts of the Piedmont — or even in March once in a while — but Jack Frost has also been known to sneak in on the tenth or even the twentieth of the month.

What this adds up to is that the "safe" date for setting out tender flowers or vegetables without some form of protection ranges from April 10 to 25, perhaps even the 30th if you live along the northern edge of the Piedmont. For heat-lovers such as eggplant and heliotrope, which want nights to stay above 50° F, it's usually best to wait until May. Each mini-climate is different, so if you're new to the neighborhood, consult with gardeners on your block to find out what they think.

Insects

Pest control generally begins to be a problem sometime in April or early May, then gets worse in June. Since chemical pesticides have the potential to harm people, pets and the surrounding environment, you may want to begin using organic controls, though it's important to remember that organics have their own set of dangers and drawbacks.

Spray bacillus thuringiensis (Bt) on cole crops to control cabbage loopers. Try garlic and hot pepper sprays to foil flea beetles. Cover plants with nylon netting (the flimsy stuff used to make fluffy underskirts for ballet tutus) to prevent laying of eggs by squash borers, cabbage loopers, cucumber beetles, leaf miners, etc. The netting will have to be removed from most crops when they begin to bloom and require pollination by bees or other insects.

Apply sabidilla dust to kill hard-shelled beetles and bugs or use rotenone to control beetles and caterpillars that feed on leaves. Insecticidal soaps such as Safer's will get rid of aphids, spider mites, whiteflies and even some thrips and sawflies. Some organic dusts and sprays also contain copper to help control fungal diseases.

Vigorous plants usually resist insect attack better than weak ones, so raise healthy vegetables by picking a site with plenty of sun, using copious amounts of compost, applying appropriate fertilizers, thinning to proper distances, watering during dry periods, and mulching with organic materials such as partially rotted hay or a mix of half-rotted, chopped leaves plus lawn clippings.

If you want to read up on organic controls, a good book with which to start is: Rodale's Garden Insect, Disease and Weed Identification Guide (Emmaus, PA; Rodale Press; 1988; $21.95). A free, very helpful mail-order catalog of organic controls can be ordered by sending your name and address to: Gardens Alive!, 5100 Schenley Place, Lawrenceburg, IN. 47041.

Poison ivy, poison oak

Kill these unwanted invaders now, just as they're beginning to put out fresh, rapidly growing leaves. Young plants can be uprooted by hand and disposed of, but older plants call for the use of an herbicide. Apply the liquid to leaves with a sprayer or by hand. (Put on a rubber glove and slip a cloth glove over the rubber. Dip into herbicide and rub it on the leaves).

Lawns

Fescue and bluegrass should have been fed in February or early March, but reseeding can be done until the middle of the month.

Feed warm-season grasses such as Bermuda, centipede and zoysia toward the end of the month — or in early May — as they begin to green up. In general, apply 15 to 25 pounds of complete fertilizer per 5,000 square feet of lawn.

During late April and continuing well into May, many nurseries offer seed, sod and plugs of various warm-season grasses. These can be used to start new lawns or patch bare spots. Prepare ground carefully beforehand and water new plantings frequently.

Broadleaf weeds on lawns can be killed with the use of various herbicides now on the market. Any herbicide is potentially dangerous to both you and the environment, so weigh that against the benefits to be derived.

One major problem with broadleaf weed killers is that they are lethal to clover. Lawns of bluegrass or fescue that have stands of clover in them tend to be healthier than one-grass lawns, so killing off the clover along with dandelions and plantain is really counterproductive. The two best alternatives, then, may be digging out unwanted weeds by hand or carefully applying an herbicide on a weed-by-weed basis.

Shrubs and trees

Prune spring-flowering shrubs as their blossoms fade (or while they're in bloom if you want to use the flowers indoors). Avoid carving these shrubs into hard balls or shearing off their tops to ugly flatness. Instead, try to accentuate their naturally graceful shapes by careful removal of just a few unwanted limbs.

With forsythia, quince, winter jasmine and other multi-trunked shrubs, cut off a few of the older, central stems right at ground level so new trunks can spring up and take over. Prune azaleas by snipping back awkwardly long branches that have just a ring of foliage at the top but little along the length of the stem.

If you didn't prune nandinas in the winter because the berries were so pretty, do it now while the bushes are at their ugliest. Snip off the old berries, but don't cut back the top of the bush. Instead, as with forsythia, cut a third of the old canes off at ground level.

Azaleas

Fertilize bushes after blooms have faded if they weren't fed last month. Container-grown azaleas are offered for sale in great numbers during April, and this is a reasonably good time to buy them simply because it's easy to tell exactly what color the blossoms are. It's also easy to kill newly planted azaleas by exposing them to hostile conditions, so take these steps to ensure survival:

Pick a sheltered site in the partial shade of tall deciduous trees or evergreens. Avoid western exposures that receive full afternoon sun.

Prepare the ground by digging up soil and mixing in a three- to four-inch layer of peat moss, leaf compost and/or finely ground bark. If possible, have the soil tested beforehand so you can adjust the pH to suit the azaleas (they like slightly acid soil with a pH of 5.0 to 5.5). Just before planting, mix a slow-release shrub fertilizer, azalea food or cottonseed meal into the earth.

Remove azaleas from pot and loosen soil ball to let roots spread out. Azaleas demand good drainage and have a very shallow root system that mustn't be smothered, so place shrub in prepared earth at exactly the same depth as it grew in the pot or even an inch shallower.

Mulch lightly with pine needles or shredded bark. Water thoroughly after planting and plan to water twice a week during the coming hot months. More azaleas die of lack of water during their first summer than for any other reason.

Bamboo

New shoots will poke up through the ground this month. Use a machete or hatchet to cut off unwanted sprouts, severing them as far below the soil surface as possible.

To experiment with eating fresh bamboo, blanch a shoot by mounding earth over it the very day it emerges. When the sprout is a foot high, remove the soil and cut off the sprout below ground level, then consult an Oriental cookbook.

Vines

Cut down old fronds of Japanese climbing fern (Lygodium) to make way for new shoots. Feed lightly or mulch with finished compost.

After the last frost, sow seeds of tender vines, including balloon, morning glory, scarlet runner, hyacinth bean, cardinal, cypress and Japanese hop. Also set out transplants of both annual and perennial vines, from clematis and trumpet creeper to black-eyed Susan (Thunbergia).

Feed Carolina jessamine after flowers have faded. Also apply a light dose of fertilizer to star jasmine and common white jasmine.

Roses

Bushes don't need to be fed in April if they were fertilized at the end of March. If you delayed, feed them during the first week of the month. Continue spraying or dusting as necessary.

Spring bulbs

Many flowering bulbs decorate gardens this month. To ensure they bloom again next spring, pick off fading flowers but leave the foliage alone. Allow the leaves to mature naturally and remove them only after they have turned yellow in late May or early June.

Some gardeners like to apply fertilizer as the blossoms fade, especially if they failed to feed the bulbs in January. This may work with plants such as crocuses, daffodils and hyacinths, but it has been shown to encourage fusarium wilt in tulips.

Forced bulbs

Gift pots of flowering bulbs (daffodils, Easter lilies, etc.) can be planted outside after the flowers fade. If lifted gently from the pot so the soil and roots aren't disturbed, their foliage should mature naturally, and the bulbs may well bloom in the garden next year.

Summer bulbs and tubers

Although instructions may suggest you set them out after all danger of frost has passed, it's actually fine to plant most of these dormant bulbs and tubers early in the month, including dahlia, canna, crinum, crocosmia, tuberose and all sorts of lilies. If bulbs are already growing in pots and have aboveground leaves that could be killed by low temperatures, then it is important to wait until no further frost is expected.

A few bulbs, like caladiums, absolutely insist upon warm soil, and you must wait a few more weeks to plant them outside.

One trait virtually all bulbs have in common is their need for good drainage. Prepare the soil by loosening it to at least ten inches and working in a substantial quantity of organic matter. Also add a low nitrogen fertilizer that has plenty of phosphorus (perhaps a commercial 5-10-5). If the food is an organic with low phosphorus (maybe 5-3-4), supplement it with two cups of bone meal per 100 square feet or a sprinkling of superphosphate.

It is also time to dig, divide and replant any cannas or dahlias that were left in the ground over the winter.

This isn't absolutely mandatory for most cannas, but dahlias usually do better with this treatment, especially if the ground is enriched with compost and fertilizer before the divisions are replanted.

Begin making plantings every two weeks of gladiolus bulbs to supply cut flowers throughout the summer. Sprinkle bulb fertilizer over the bottom of the hole and cover with an inch of soil, then put the bulb in and finish filling in the hole.

Tuberous begonias don't really like our hot summers, but they may perform acceptably if given homes in large pots on the north side of a house where sun rarely shines. The soil must stay moist but not sink into sogginess, and the plants often respond well to frequent feedings with an organic liquid, such as compost or manure tea or fish emulsion.

Geraniums

Whether purchased, grown at home from cuttings or revived after being stored for the winter, all types of geraniums can be set out into the garden after the last frost.

Perennial and biennial flowers

These plants are not affected by late cold snaps and so can be set out right away. If you own a good reference book on perennials, try to take it with you when visiting nurseries and read about unfamiliar plants before buying them. See March notes for ground preparation.

Don't be fooled into thinking that delphiniums, primroses and other cool-climate perennials are going to do well in most of the Piedmont. They may bloom this year, but it's doubtful they'll live through a second year except in the coolest gardens. If you must have delphiniums, see the September notes for a suggestion about growing them as annuals.

Chrysanthemums and perennial salvia (mealy-cup sage) may continue from year to year with no special attention, but they usually do much better if the old clump is dug up now and divided. Discard most of the gnarled, woody parts and separate new growth into several smaller pieces, each with some roots attached. Replant in rich soil and water with a weak solution of fish emulsion or root stimulator.

Annual flowers

Annuals that are hardy enough to be planted outside right at the start of April include pansies, petunias, alyssum, annual foxglove, calendula and snapdragons. Really, it's hardly worth planting pansies or calendula except in the coolest areas because they loathe hot weather. Better to wait until fall.

Tender annuals, a category that includes the majority of bedding plants for sale at nurseries and garden centers, shouldn't be placed in the garden until the last half of the month, including ageratum, wax begonia, marigold, portulaca, coleus, cockscomb (Celosia), cosmos, zinnia, strawflower, impatiens, burning bush and vinca.

If you decide to second-guess Mother Nature and set them out early, be sure to have protection on hand (row covers, bottomless milk jugs, etc.) for frosty nights.

Wait until late April or early May, if you can, to set out transplants of flowers that like to have nights above 50°F, including arctotis, flowering maple, amaranth, heliotrope and zinnia.

Plant seeds of most tender annuals after the middle of April. These include cockscomb, cleome, cosmos, portulaca, marigold, nasturtium, sunflower and four o'clocks. If seeds need especially warm soil to germinate, it may be wise to wait a week or two longer, depending on local temperatures.

To protect newly planted seeds, retain moisture, encourage even germination and prevent washout by heavy rain, cover seeded areas with a porous floating row cover or burlap. Keep soil moist by watering through the cover. Burlap must be removed as soon as seeds germinate, but a floating row cover can stay in place for a couple of weeks longer, until seedlings are off to a good start.

Herbs

Hardy herbs, like parsley, thyme and chives, can be set out any time, and dill seeds can be sown throughout the month.

Overwintered parsley may be bothered by brown caterpillars which chew through the stems at the base of the plant. Spray with Bt to control this problem. Parsley is a biennial, which means that last year's plants will eventually bloom and die later in the spring. To ensure a steady supply of leaves, you must either set out new plants or sow seeds now.

Seeds of tender herbs, like basil and coriander, shouldn't be sown until after the last frost, nor should transplants be set out.

Vegetables

Transplants of all sorts are available for sale during April. Trouble is, the best selection and the lowest prices are often found early in the month, yet the ideal planting weather for many of them is not until the end of the month.

One way to cope with this disparity is to buy the plants in early April and then put them in a cold frame until the weather is warm (replant in larger containers if you must hold them for more than a week). Another is to protect tender plants with floating row covers, cloches, hotcaps or heat-retention devices such as Wall'O'Water.

At the start of the month, thin lettuce, carrots, turnips and other crowded crops to proper spacing. When potato foliage is about six inches tall, hill soil up around it so that only the top couple of leaves can be seen.

Harvest or pull up and compost most of the remaining over-wintered crops, such as kale, spinach and collards, as they begin to bolt.

After six weeks' worth of harvesting asparagus spears, it's time to stop. Nourish the plants by feeding with two to three pounds of fertilizer per 100 square feet. Weed if necessary. Mulch thickness should be three to six inches, so apply more if necessary.

As Jerusalem artichoke leaves emerge late in the month, spread a thin layer of finished compost or bagged manure over the plot to supply nutrients for the coming year.

When carrot plantings are six weeks old, add an inch of fine compost or a mix of ¾ sifted soil and ¼ dried manure to the bed. This will gently fertilize the carrots and also shade the root tops from the sun, keeping them sweeter.

Unless vegetables planted in February and March are in extremely fertile ground enriched with plenty of compost, you'll need to feed most of them every two to three weeks. It is often easiest to use manure tea, fish emulsion, rotted manure or liquid fertilizer on small plants. Larger ones can be given liquids too, or you can side-dress them with one to three tablespoons of granular fertilizer, organic or not.

April 1-15, set out transplants of semi-hardy vegetables, including celery and Swiss chard. It's too late for broccoli and cauliflower, even though they may be for sale, so don't try. Make another planting of beets and carrots. Plant corn if desired but protect it with a row covering until the end of the month.

Scarlet runner beans can be planted in mid-April and will sprout in cool soil, but don't expect much of a crop. Although the vines should flower decoratively all summer, they absolutely refuse to set beans during hot weather.

April 16-30, set out most tender vegetable transplants, including cantaloupe, cucumber, Malabar spinach, summer squash, tomato, watermelon and zucchini. If weather is unseasonably cool, wait until the first week of May.

Plant seeds of warm-weather vegetables such as green beans (bush and half-runner), cantaloupe, corn, cucumber, summer squash and zucchini. After the 20th, or later if soil has not warmed sufficiently, plant seeds of gourd, luffa and watermelon.

Indoor seedlings, April 1-7, start seeds of cantaloupe, okra and peppers. During the first two weeks of April begin hardening off transplants that will go outside during the last two weeks of the month.

Fruit

Set out alpine strawberry plants during the first half of the month. Feed new beds of strawberry plants which were set out in January, February or March. Pick off any flowers that form on these new plants.

Place bird netting over established strawberry beds just after they begin flowering. Slugs often do much of the damage attributed to birds, so consider putting out bait or traps to control these pests as the fruits form.

Continue with the fruit-tree spraying schedule you decided on in March, including, perhaps, a fungal spray for cherries and plums.

House plants

House plants probably shouldn't go outside until May unless they are on a sheltered balcony or near a heat-retaining wall. In the meantime, continue to water and fertilize regularly.

Shift light-lovers closer to windows; the angle of the sun is changing rapidly right now, and its rays don't shine as deeply into south windows as they used to.

Notes

May

Nights become warmer during May and the growing season is under way in earnest. In dry years there may not be enough rain each week to keep things going, so extra watering of annuals, vegetables, lawns and ornamental shrubs is often necessary. An inch of water a week is the usual rule, but well-established shrubs and trees will need less while newly planted items, productive vegetables and flowering perennials and annuals may require more.

Japanese beetles

These gaudy beetles are a big problem in some areas, especially suburbs where there are large lawn areas (the larvae live below ground and munch on grass roots). The best long-term control is spraying with milky spore disease. Lawns for several miles around must be sprayed to be effective, so you'll have to organize the neighbors.

It will be a couple of years after spraying before the disease cuts down on the number of beetles in the neighborhood. In the meantime, knock clusters of beetles into pails of soapy water, protect rose blossoms and grape clusters by covering with nylon net or old stockings and apply an insecticide like rotenone to vulnerable flowers and vegetables.

Scented traps have mixed results since they kill some beetles but may attract hordes of others to the area without actually trapping them. If you use traps, place on a corner of your property away from vegetable and flower areas.

Lawns

Warm-season grasses turn fully green in May. If they weren't fed last month, fertilize at the start of the month. Sod and seed of Bermuda, centipede and zoysia are available for patching bare areas and starting new lawns in areas that receive full sun.

Don't start lawns of cool-season grasses from seed if you can avoid it; they won't have enough time to become established before hot weather. A quick but expensive alternative is to buy fescue sod, though it'll require plenty of water for the rest of the summer.

All lawns need regular mowing. Use a mulching mower so clippings can be left in place to decompose or collect the clippings and compost them.

Warning: if a weed-killer or pre-emergent crabgrass preventer was used on the lawn, don't compost the clippings since the chemicals may hang around in the compost long enough to affect flowers or vegetables.

Shrubs and trees

To prevent damage to trees and shrubs while mowing and to keep roots protected from moisture loss, surround them with a ring of mulch. Start the ring a few inches away from the trunk and continue it past the drip line. Don't heap it up more than a few inches because roots can be smothered if mulch is too deep.

Shrubs and trees are usually planted during cooler weather, but those that have been grown in containers can be bought and set out in May if careful attention is paid to their need for water during the next six months.

Continue pruning spring-flowering shrubs and trees as blossoms fade, including mockorange, kerria, redbud and dogwood. Feed late azaleas after flowering finishes if you haven't already done so.

Check camellias for signs of scale insects. If present, treat with an oil spray at the dilution levels specified on the container.

If it has been a long, wet spring, check azaleas and camellias for leaf gall fungus. This fungus distorts the growth of new leaves, producing fleshy, hard, rounded galls which are light green or pink. The galls soon become chalky white with fungal spores and later turn dark brown and become hard.

The best control is to look over the plants every few days, pick off all new galls and throw them in the garbage. This will prevent spores from maturing and being blown to adjacent sites and should control the problem within a few weeks. If the fungus spreads too widely, you may need to use a fungicidal spray in combination with the picking.

Vines

Set out transplants of heat-loving annual vines like moonflower and tropical perennials like mandevillea. Seeds of morning glory and other fast-growing vines can be planted outside any time.

This is a good time to prune many vines that have finished blooming for the year, like akebia and Carolina jessamine. You should also remove faded blooms from clematis and lightly trim trumpet honeysuckle to encourage another flush of flowers later in the year.

Prune wisteria heavily at the start of the month and then feed.

Roses

Feed bushes at the start of the month. Continue spraying or dusting routines as necessary. Cut off dead flowers to encourage new ones.

Spring bulbs

Leaves of spring-flowering bulbs may begin to mature in late May, but not all varieties will be fully yellow until June. See June's notes for cutting and overplanting.

Summer bulbs

Continue planting gladiolus bulbs every couple of weeks. Plant canna lilies, crinums, dahlias, tuberose (Polianthes), ginger lilies and other heat-loving bulbs. See April notes for tuberous begonias. Caladiums love warm soil and can usually be planted outside by mid-May.

Datura

Angels trumpets that have been grown from seed or cuttings can be planted now that the weather is stable. When planted in fertile soil in a sheltered location and mulched in late fall, datura roots will often survive Piedmont winters and resprout in the spring.

Fuschia

Pots and hanging baskets filled with these ballerina-skirt blossoms are a great temptation in late April and early May. But beware. It is very hard to keep a fuschia happy because it wants cool, misty weather instead of the hot, sunny stuff that characterizes our summers.

Buy one if you must, but put it in a spot that gets only a bit of morning sun and is cool and shaded in the afternoon. Be prepared to water and mist the foliage nearly every day and don't be too surprised if it sulks and refuses to continue blooming after a few weeks.

Perennial flowers

Regular deadheading (cutting off faded flowers) promotes the formation of new buds on repeat bloomers and helps plants begin to store energy for next year. It is still fine to buy and set out perennial flowers, but be sure to water them regularly.

Start pinching back tall chrysanthemums every two weeks to produce shorter, stockier plants with more blossoms. If you prefer taller plants with just a few large terminal buds, stake plants as necessary and do not pinch.

Stake tall plants that have heavy flower spikes so that wind or rain won't blow them over.

Annual flowers

Transplants can be set out anytime this month, including the heat-lovers like arctotis, amaranth, zinnia, geraniums, winged everlastings, coleus, heliotrope, vinca and flowering maple. Set them out on a cloudy day or in early evening so they have some hours without direct sun to adapt to their new home.

All sorts of annual seeds can be sown directly in the garden, including marigolds, cleome, vinca, cosmos, zinnia, sunflower, nasturtium, cockscomb (celosia), portulaca and annual phlox. Read about each variety before planting to make sure it will reach flowering size in a reasonable amount of time. Some annuals grow so slowly that it is better to set them out as transplants. These include impatiens, petunia, torenia, snapdragon and penstemon.

Toward the end of the month look for volunteer seedlings of impatiens, vinca, cleome and other annuals. Dig and transplant as desired.

Avoid planting annuals that prefer cool weather, like calendula, pansies, ornamental kale, Himalayan blue poppy and blue lace flower. Some of these can be used in early spring or in the fall, but planting them in May is sure to bring disappointment.

Herbs

Set out herb transplants any time during the month and plant seeds of annuals like basil and summer savory.

Cut chives back to the ground as they begin blooming (or after flowers fade if you like the decorative touch brought to your garden by the round lavender flowers). This will get rid of all the woody flower stems and stimulate tender new growth. Water and fertilize lightly after cutting back.

Succulent herbs, like parsley, chives, mint and basil, need plenty of water and some fertilizer. Tough perennial herbs like rosemary and thyme need less water and no synthetic fertilizer, though they may appreciate a light top-dressing of finished compost or other organic food.

Vegetables

Water vegetables on a regular basis. Most should be fertilized every two to three weeks with liquid food, foliar sprays or a side-dressing of chemical or organic granules.

Hill up soil around leaves of white potatoes at the start of the month as you did in April. Feed the plants as you work, with about two cups of 5-10-10 or equivalent organic formula per 25 feet of row or a tablespoon of fertilizer per plant.

Continue setting out transplants of warm weather vegetables and melons, including cantaloupe, Malabar or New Zealand spinach, summer squash, tomatoes and watermelon. Once nights are continuously above 50° F and soil is warm (above 65° F), set out transplants of eggplant, all sorts of peppers and also sweet potato slips.

Seeds of a number of warm-weather vegetables can be planted any time this month, including lima bean, bush bean, pole beans of all kinds (even Chinese yard-long), cantaloupe, watermelon, honeydew, cucumber, gourd and summer squashes. Wait until after the middle of the month (or until soil temperature is above 65°F) to plant seeds of pumpkin, peanuts, soy beans, Southern peas and okra. Soak okra seeds in tepid water for 24 hours before planting to speed germination.

Although winter squash will grow if planted now, it's better to wait until late June if you want fruit for winter storage (rinds on fruits from later plantings are thicker and tougher than those from early sowings).

Most overwintered crops, such as kale, collards and spinach, should be pulled out and composted early in the month if not done last month. Cut bloom spikes off any remaining leeks so they will have plenty of energy to produce extra mini-bulbs. These bulbs can be pulled up and replanted in the fall.

May usually spells the end of spring lettuce because it turns bitter and starts to bolt toward the end of the month. You may want to experiment with planting seeds of heat-resistant strains in a moist, partially shaded area.

Turnips and radishes should be harvested and used before they become pithy and unpleasant. Radish seed pods are tasty if picked while young and steamed or stir-fried; if you haven't overwintered a couple of fall radishes for that purpose, leave a few spring radishes in place so they can bloom. Keep an eye out for harlequin bugs which love to munch on the flowers. Knock the adults off into soapy water during the early morning hours when they are still cold and clumsy or dust the babies with a mild pesticide as soon as they hatch out.

Broccoli, cauliflower and cabbage should be mulched at the start of the month to keep the soil cool. Check frequently for caterpillars and dust with Bt as necessary. Broccoli will continue to put out side shoots after the main head is harvested. Pick and use these until hot weather makes them bitter; then pull plants and compost.

Blanch cauliflower by clothes pinning a couple of side leaves over the heads. Pick both cauliflower and cabbage before they start to bolt; harvested heads will keep in the refrigerator for up to six weeks.

When green, sugar snap and snow peas begin bearing, pick pods every couple of days to keep more coming. If cool weather (under 60°F) causes early tomatoes to fail to set fruit, spray with a blossom-set solution.

Fruit

Continue spraying summer and fall fruit trees on schedule. Do not spray cherry trees after the first week of May since you'll be harvesting early varieties at the end of the month. Protect ripening fruits from bird attack by covering strawberry beds and small trees with bird netting or even floating row cover material. Hold in place with clothespins for easy removal later. Try noise devices, mylar ribbons or inflatable plastic snakes and owls on larger trees.

Thin peaches and plums if necessary so fruits are about four inches apart.

Look for fire blight on pear and apple trees. Cut off affected branches below the end of the dead portion. Dip pruning shears in bleach between cuttings to disinfect them. Burn prunings or put in garbage can.

Feed early strawberries after they have stopped producing new berries. Fertilize pecan trees that were planted this past winter. If established nut trees have a heavy nutset, feed them, too, at the end of the month.

House plants

Put your babies outside after the start of the month, when nights are warm on a regular basis. This change is always a shock, so start plants out in fairly deep shade and move into brighter sun little by little over the course of a couple of weeks.

Few of your house plants will want full sun all day, though bougainvillea, cacti, dwarf pomegranate and citrus trees do need several hours' worth. Most of the others prefer partial to deep shade for the whole summer, including African violet, streptocarpus, ficus tree, Boston and Dallas ferns, cyclamen, philodendron, orchid and all of the rex begonias.

Containers can be kept above the ground, on a porch or patio, or actually plunged into the earth with just the rim of the pot visible. If they are buried in this manner, cover drainage holes with porous landscape cloth so that roots won't grow through holes into the ground below and worms can't work their way into the potting soil. Shake the plant out of its pot, pop a circle of landscape cloth into place, then put the plant back in its pot.

Jerusalem cherries need partial to full sun and can be kept in pots or planted in the ground to grow during the summer. Sometimes they will live through the winter, especially if heavily mulched, but don't count on it.

Poinsettias need frequent watering and fertilization. Once nights are reliably above 50°F, set them in a lightly shaded spot (full sun would scald the leaves). Amaryllis bulbs can stay in pots or be planted outside permanently. Although reference books say these bulbs are hardy only to zone 8, many zone 7 gardeners keep them outside year after year with great success. Plant the bulbs several inches below the surface of the soil in a sunny, well-drained spot. If you prefer to keep the bulbs in pots for re-blooming next winter, set them in partial to full sun, water frequently and feed regularly. They won't look pretty but the leaves will work hard at storing up energy for next year.

Notes

June

   Although daffodils are long gone, most peonies have shed their lovely petals and spring lettuce tastes unbearably bitter, June has its own special gifts to offer. Early tomatoes ripen this month and magnolia trees are laden with lemon-scented blossoms. Days are much hotter now and gardeners must often resort to working outside only in the early morning or late afternoon.

   June is usually the month when rains stop and the dry season begins. Regular watering, at least once a week, is needed in most gardens and mulches are vital to help conserve moisture.

Insects

Pests are always a problem in the summer, so take another look at the April and May notes. Keep an eye out for yellow jackets; they often build nests under lawns or inside wooden landscape ties and may attack while you're mowing or walking through the yard. Look for small holes where these fliers are taking off and landing, then spray it at night with a wasp and hornet killer. That should kill the whole nest since all the yellow jackets will be asleep inside.

Pouring gasoline into the hole and then covering the opening with soil may also work but is a bit dangerous and can injure neighboring plants.

Also be on the lookout for tomato hornworms which often appear in June or July. They are green caterpillars marked with diagonal stripes and a black "horn" at the rear. Hornworms may grow up to four inches long and can eat plenty of tomato foliage in just one day. They look fierce but do not bite or sting, so handpick and crush or just cut them in half with scissors. If you can see hornworms that have little white eggs or cocoons attached, leave them be. These hold beneficial parasitic wasps that will shortly kill the hornworm. By allowing the parasites to live, you will help prevent future problems in the garden.

Green caterpillars that are striped or dotted in black and orange may appear on parsley, fennel or carrot foliage. Each will eventually form a green chrysalis from which a gorgeous black or yellow swallowtail butterfly will emerge. Some gardeners, and I'm definitely one of them, are willing to sacrifice a few plants so that these winged beauties can survive.

Lawns

Grasses of all kinds grow lushly and require regular mowing. Set mower high for fescue and other cool-weather grasses so the longer blades of grass will shade the ground and keep it cooler. Deep watering of fescue and newly planted centipede is mandatory in weeks that have less than an inch of rain.

Shrubs and trees

June and July are considered the best months in which to take softwood cuttings from many shrubs, including azaleas and camellias. Root the cuttings in a moist, shaded location using a half-and-half mix of sand and peat moss.

Feed gumpo azaleas after they finish blooming. Prune lightly to keep a softly mounded, natural shape.

It is possible to plant container-grown shrubs and trees this month but not so easy to keep them alive. Better to wait until fall unless you're desperate and can water twice a week.

Vines

Plant morning glory seeds, as well as those of other fast-growing annual vines, if not already done. Renew the compost mulch on clematis if it has thinned and remove fading flowers unless you want seedheads to form.

Roses

Feed as usual this month and continue routine maintenance as necessary, including spraying, watering and deadheading.

Prune climbers and ramblers that flower only once as soon as blooms fade, removing old canes to ground level and partially cutting back new canes if they are too long for the trellis. Some climbers bloom on and off during the summer on new branches produced all along the older stems; thin these out as necessary to keep these plants neat and within bounds.

June is also a good time to give each rose bush a half-cup of lime, just as you did (or will do) in January.

Spring bulbs

The leaves of most spring bulbs finish maturing now, turn yellow and can be cut back to ground level. Dig up crowded bulbs, especially tulips, and break off small bulblets which have formed. Replant (but do not fertilize) larger bulbs; discard smaller ones unless you want to grow them to blooming size, which may take two years.

To provide summer and fall color, overplant spring bulb areas with annual transplants or seeds.

Order bulbs for fall planting from catalogs or local garden clubs. Most catalogs offer a discount on bulbs ordered by June 15, so take advantage of these lower prices if you can. The bulbs will be delivered in October or early November, just in time for planting.

Summer bulbs

Tubers of caladium, canna, elephant ear and dahlia can still be planted, though they won't be as immediately attractive as those bulbs that have been growing in pots for a couple of months.

Stake tall lilies before they begin to bloom.

Set out two more rounds of gladiolus bulbs, spacing them a couple of weeks apart. Clip off amaryllis blooms (but not the leaves!) after they've faded.

Perennial flowers

Continue to cut faded blooms and feed most perennials lightly at the start of the month (especially the ones that will bloom later in the summer). As described in the May notes, pinch back tall chrysanthemums once or twice this month to make them bushier.

Bearded iris clumps that have become crowded can be lifted and divided this month. Cut leaves back by half as you do so to minimize water loss after transplanting.

Prune dying flowers from peonies. Feed by mulching with a gallon of finished compost mixed with a ½ cup wood ashes and a tablespoon of bonemeal. If that's not possible, apply a quarter-cup of 5-10-10 or a ¼ cup of organic granules plus a tablespoon of bonemeal.

Annual flowers

It's not too late to sow seeds of many annual flowers, including zinnia, cosmos, nasturtium, ganzania, annual phlox, cleome, sanvitalia, celosia and sunflowers.

Established plants need regular fertilizing, deadheading and watering to keep the blooms coming. Scratch in a ½ cup of organic or chemical granules per square yard of soil or water with liquid food. A mulch of bark, grass clippings or other organic material will help retain soil moisture and keep most annuals much happier.

Pansies begin to look ratty in the heat, so pull up and discard. Replace with transplants or seeds of fast-growing summer annuals.

As you did in late May, look around for self-sown seedlings from impatiens, cleome, vinca and other annuals which grew in your garden last year. Leave them where they are or transplant as desired.

Petunias should probably be trimmed back toward the end of the month to keep them bushy and encourage formation of new flowers. Feed and water after the pruning.

Herbs

Although it may seem early, many herbs should be cut for drying at the start of June, before they bloom and lose flavor, including basil, thyme and mint. Dill can be chopped, mixed with water and frozen into cubes in ice trays. To use, drop cube into soup, sauce, etc., and let it melt.

Make a new planting of basil seeds for late summer use.

Vegetables

Green peas wither and die in the June heat. Pull them up and compost, along with other cool-weather crops that are dying back or have become too bitter to eat. Pea vines can be used as mulch around bramble fruits, something they seem to love.

Harvest beans and other crops as they ripen. Continue to fertilize, weed and water all vegetables as necessary.

Dig onions and garlic when the tops turn yellow and fall over; let dry in a well-ventilated space before storing. Gather baby walking onions (sometimes called Egyptian onions) from the mother plants as stalks begin to weaken and fall over. Store these bulblets indoors in a dry, cool spot until it's time to plant them in the fall for winter scallions.

White potatoes may begin to die back at the end of the month; if so, dig, dry and store. Prompt handling is vital, so as soon as they're dug, dry them for just a few hours in the shade, then move indoors to a dark place with reasonably high humidity and a temperature range of 55° to 60° F.

When white potatoes are exposed to sunlight for more than a few hours, or are left out in the rain, half or more of them may rot during the first few weeks of storage (I'm speaking from sad experience here).

If potatoes can be stored in the dark at 40° F, which is difficult to do during the summer, they will keep for up to eight months. At normal room temperatures, they will usually keep for six to eight weeks.

June 1-15, set out sweet potato slips if not done in May. Make first or second planting of soy beans, pole beans, bush beans, Southern peas, pumpkins, cantaloupe, okra, and summer squash. Make a last planting of sweet corn.

June 16-30, plant seeds of winter squash for fruits with tough rinds that will store well after harvest. Plant pumpkin seeds now for harvest in October, just in time for Halloween. Continue to sow seeds of cantaloupe, okra and Southern peas.

Seedlings: June 1-15, start transplants of eggplant, pepper and tomato for setting out in July to yield a heavy fall crop. For best germination and early growth, sow seeds in a partially shaded seedbed or flat.

You can also break off suckers from established tomato plants and root them in moist potting soil to produce large transplants quite quickly.

Fruit

Feed late strawberries after the last fruits have been picked. Feed everbearing and alpine strawberries to encourage continued production. Water is necessary for juicy fruits and the alpines will taste perfectly awful without plenty of it.

Rejuvenate old, crowded strawberry beds. There are several ways of doing this: One method is to pull out old plants and then respace the younger ones. Another is to move young, rooted runners to an entirely new plot and then compost the old plants. Wait until fall, after the final harvest, to destroy old plants of everbearing varieties.

Continue with spray schedule on fruits that won't ripen until fall. If peaches or plums turned brown last summer just before ripening, they were probably infected with brown rot. Help prevent this from happening again by spraying with sulfur or other fruit fungicides about three weeks before the fruit usually ripens. Also pick up and dispose of fallen fruit so spores won't have a place to grow.

Fertilize bearing grapes, both bunch and muscadine, with a dose of organic liquid fertilizer like manure tea or fish emulsion. Cover ripening blueberries with bird netting. After the middle of the month, begin applying a gallon or so of water to the soil around each blueberry bush every evening, unless there is plenty of rain. Ample water is critical to the formation of plump berries.

Toward month's end, protect grape clusters, pears, apples, etc. from insect or bird damage with netting or by covering each cluster or fruit with a brown paper bag or a perforated plastic bag (the kind used to wrap hot bakery bread). Or sew your own bags from the nylon netting used to make ballet tutus. These can be used for several years if taken inside for storage immediately after harvest so that exposure to sunlight is minimized. Twist-tie or tape the bag tops to hold in place.

House plants

Plants that are spending the summer outside require continued watering plus regular feeding. Indoor plants need good air circulation to help prevent mold and mildew diseases. If your house isn't air conditioned, place plants near an open window or in a room with a fan that is turned on once or twice a day. Also make sure their individual needs for light are met.

Cyclamen seed can be planted in June for bloom in seven to eighteen months, depending on the variety (just in case you want to try a long-term project).

July

Sizzling heat and few rains combine to make July a difficult month for most Piedmont Plateau gardeners. Nevertheless, well-tended gardens will yield bountiful crops of midsummer vegetables and flowers to reward those who persevere.

Many spring-blooming weeds disperse their seeds in July. Prevent future problems by weeding garden areas thoroughly early in the month. Dispose of seed-bearing weeds unless they can be composted in a really hot pile.

Rapidly drying soil may crust around the bases of plants and can injure soft stems. Crusted soil may also resist moisture penetration and cause water from rains or sprinklers to run off. Mulch soil to prevent crusting; use a cultivator or hoe to break up hard soil where mulching is impossible.

Although it seems that fall will never come, transplants of some flowers and vegetables must be started in July to be ready for setting out in August and September.

Lawns

Bermuda seed or sprigs can be planted in July since this is a real heat-loving grass.

Fescue and bluegrass may look pretty ratty now, so keep them cut on the long side (three or four inches). Water weekly if possible, applying a full inch during the cool hours of morning or evening when the least amount of moisture will evaporate. Contrary to previous notions, evening watering does not seem to increase the incidence of fungal diseases nor will watering in sunlight "burn" the grass.

Warm-season grasses tolerate drought reasonably well, but even they may benefit from a deep watering every two or three weeks if absolutely no rain falls. Grasses that were seeded or started by sodding this spring will need more water than well-established lawns.

Shrubs and trees

Cut fading flowers from crape myrtles and vitex trees to encourage formation of new blooms. Trim off suckers as they appear near the base or on lower trunk(s) of various ornamental trees.

Prune ball-type hydrangeas as blooms fade. Many varieties will bloom again if fed lightly now and watered regularly. To save some of the huge clusters for winter bouquets, cut the flowers when they are stiff and have begun to dry on their own but before the color has completely faded. Remove leaves. Stick them in a basket or empty vase indoors and they will finish drying into attractive silver-beige globes.

Vines

Cut new shoots on wisteria back by half to keep vine in bounds and encourage better blooming next year.

Roses

Roses may stop growing and take a rest during super-hot weather, especially those that are in full sun all day. Water deeply at least once a week and spray as necessary but do not feed this month unless plants are growing vigorously and seem to need it. Prune off faded flowers and cut back any weak growth to get plant ready for a long blooming spell in the fall.

Perennial and biennial flowers

Pinch chrysanthemums back for the last time this month and feed them lightly, along with any other perennials that haven't blossomed. Feed re-blooming daylilies after the first flush of flowers has faded and give peonies a gentle midsummer dose of fish emulsion or liquid kelp.

Divide and reset crowded bearded irises if not already done. Mark positions of perennials whose foliage will soon die back, like bleeding heart and Oriental poppy, so you won't dig them up by mistake.

Use pieces of concrete reinforcing wire, sturdy tree branches with plenty of side stems or several stakes plus zigzagging pieces of string to keep bushy perennials like tall mealycup sage and hardy ageratum from flopping over as the stems lengthen.

Most biennials should be started from seed in July, including foxglove, sweet William, hollyhock, Canterbury bells and money plant (lunaria). Also start annual foxglove since it does best if treated as a biennial in this climate. Seedlings will be ready to transplant to the garden in early fall.

July is also a good time to sow seeds of many perennials. Try newly ripened seed from things already in the garden as well as purchased seeds of columbine, daylily, gaillardia, blackberry lily, Park's candy lily, butterfly weed, Lenten rose, Shasta daisy, aster, coneflower (Echinacea), veronica, rudbeckia and others.

Plant perennial and biennial seeds in flats, pots or in a specially prepared seedbed in partial shade. Keep soil evenly moist. Some gardeners like to start the plants indoors under lights because an air-conditioned house may be easier on seedlings than the hot outdoors.

Annual flowers

Constant deadheading, regular fertilization and plenty of water will encourage continued production of new flowers. Stake tall plants such as sunflowers and giant cosmos. Cut back leggy petunias, snapdragons and other annuals; apply liquid fertilizer afterward.

A late planting of fast-growing zinnias, marigolds, annual asters, etc. can be made at the start of July for blooms in August and September.

As you pull out dying larkspur, poppies or Johnny jump-up at the start of the month, shake plants over the soil so the seeds will fall out and self-sow. Even better, especially if the area will be overplanted, shake the plants over a layer of newspaper, dry, save and then plant the seeds outdoors in the fall or late winter.

Seeds of hardy annuals that bloom in the fall and early winter can be started this month, including pansies, alyssum and ornamental kale and cabbage. Calendula can also be tried in the warmest areas though it really does best as a fall or winter annual slightly farther south.

Herbs

Plant basil seeds for a fall crop. Continue to cut and dry herbs for winter use.

Make herbal vinegars by placing a sprig or two of tarragon, basil or oregano in a jar. Fill jar with hot white vinegar and allow to steep for at least two weeks. Purple basil will produce a nice rosy hue.

Vegetables

Vegetables need the same regular watering and fertilizing that annual flowers do. Weeding is also extremely important. Pull and dispose of summer squash plants that die from borers as well as cucumbers or melons that die from beetle-transmitted wilt diseases. Burn plants or place in the garbage; do not compost plants since it is hard to get the pile to heat high enough to destroy all the grubs and diseases.

Dig and harvest white potatoes, garlic and onions if not already done (check June notes for potato storage information). Stop sweet potatoes from rooting along the length of each vine by moving the vines around a bit while weeding. If vines are allowed to root, too many small potatoes can form on the new roots and drain away energy needed to sustain the main crop of potatoes at the center of the plant.

Prune back awkwardly tall tomato plants by cutting off the top third of the growth; fertilize with foliar sprays, compost tea or other liquid food. Some experienced gardeners report that spraying tomato foliage twice monthly with a liquid calcium supplement will discourage fungal diseases as well as stave off blossom end rot.

July 1-15, plant another round of cucumbers and all sorts of beans and Southern peas plus summer squash. If desired, set out new eggplant and tomato transplants. Pull suckers off tomato plants to root and set out at the start of August. Make a first planting of some fall crops, including carrots, collards and cauliflower. Careful watering will be needed to get these up and growing.

Carrot germination will probably be better if a piece of cloth or a board is placed over the bed to keep soil cool and moist. Check daily for signs of life and remove covering as soon as you see a hint of the first skinny leaves. Another tip for encouraging good germination in hot soil is to first mix seed with damp sand and allow to sit overnight before sowing the next day.

July 16-30, continue planting carrots, summer squash, beans and Southern peas. Sow rutabagas toward the end of the month or wait until early August. Set out pepper transplants.

Seedlings: Either indoors in flats or outside in a prepared seedbed, start fall transplants of collards, cabbage, cauliflower, broccoli, onions, Brussels sprouts and celeriac.

Fruit

Grapes will be particularly vulnerable to attack by wasps and bumblebees as they begin to ripen. You may want to use one of the barrier protection methods mentioned in June.

Keep everbearing and alpine strawberries well-watered. Continue giving each blueberry bush a gallon of water a day to really plump up the berries. One efficient way to supply this water is with a drip irrigation system. A less expensive but functional alternative is to lay an old hose out in the blueberry patch under the mulch, winding it around the bushes at their driplines. Poke holes in the hose with an ice pick at appropriate spots so that water will squirt out when the faucet is turned on.

The European technique of summer pruning is especially effective on young apple trees. Read more about it in new garden books to learn the benefits and you may decide to abandon the idea of winter pruning altogether. When tender non-fruiting wood is about the thickness of a pencil, cut it back to within an inch of where it emerges from last year's wood, leaving a cluster of three to five leaves at the base. This will stimulate the formation of fruit spurs and has the added benefits of removing some aphids and dwarfing larger trees. This first pruning will remove about 75 percent of the current year's growth. Continue pruning trees in August and early September, removing other tips as they thicken to pencil size.

House plants

Check house plants that have been set outside to be sure no insects, snails, slugs or diseases have invaded. Continue regular watering and feeding. If plants placed in a sunny spot are drying out too fast, you may need to move them to partial shade, repot in larger containers and/or mix some water storage granules into the soil.

Poinsettias should be cut back by a third in July and then fed. This will produce bushier, stockier plants.

Notes

August

Like July, August is a sultry month that can try one's endurance. To avoid heatstroke, split tasks into small segments and do them a little at a time during the coolest parts of the day. Drink lots of water, wear a hat and remember the sunblock lotion.

While sitting in the shade, sipping iced tea and trying to cool off, take time to reflect on the successes and failures of the last six months. If you don't already have a garden journal, August is the perfect time to begin one because things are still fresh in your mind.

The first entry should be a summary of what has happened over the summer. Once that's done, jot down a few notes once or twice a week. This will create a record on which to base decisions for the future.

Although any old notebook will do, a well-bound book of thick, unlined pages lasts for years. Because it is blank, you can take as much or as little space as necessary for each entry. And because it has no lines, you can draw diagrams, paste in labels from unusual plants and include other oddments.

Vital information for a garden journal includes the following: Weather conditions (first and last frost, extreme temperatures, amount of rain, sleet, snow or hail), plants currently in bloom, vegetables or fruits being harvested, variety names of seeds sown and the speed of their germination, items that have been planted or transplanted, experiments in progress, insect or disease problems or solutions, soil test results, and ideas for next year. It is also wise to jot down an evaluation of the flavor and productiveness of new vegetable varieties so you'll remember whether to plant them again next year.

Lawns

Cool-season grasses still look pretty sad, but they may revive with the coming of a long rain. Mow only as necessary and continue watering on a regular basis. Wait to re-seed until the middle of September.

Warm-weather grasses are usually beautiful right now and need regular mowing. Bermuda and zoysia need a dose of slow-release fertilizer toward the end of the month to beef them up for winter survival.

Shrubs and trees

Even well-established trees and shrubs may need a good soak from time to time if rains have held off for several weeks. Shallow-rooted plants like azaleas and dogwoods are especially at risk; check soil moisture frequently if weather is dry.

August is a good month for taking hardwood cuttings from the tips of crape myrtle branches, azaleas, pieris, photinia, holly, camellia, acuba and other evergreens. Root them in a moist mix of sand and peat moss. After roots form, move cuttings to more fertile soil.

Hold off on planting new shrubs and trees until cooler weather arrives in the fall. The one exception to the no-planting rule is the crape myrtle, mainly because nurseries have a good selection of blooming specimens right now. You'll be able to pick out the color you like best, but frequent watering will, of course, be necessary after planting.

Roses

Regular watering and spraying is still important. Fertilize all ever-blooming and fall-blooming types early this month to induce a spectacular flush of flowers in September and early October.

Perennial flowers

Cut the spent blossoms from perennials that bloomed in July unless you want them to form seed for planting or because the pods are attractive enough to use in dried bouquets. Those that will flower in the fall, especially showy mums, appreciate a light feeding during the first half of the month. Keep ever-blooming daylilies like 'Stella D'Oro' and late re-bloomers happy by feeding at the start of the month and watering deeply if soil is dry.

Divide Japanese iris if needed.

Cuttings of some perennials can be taken now, rooted, and set out in October. These include carnation, phlox, sedum and pinks. There's still time to start perennials and biennials from seeds if you didn't do it in July.

For spectacular football and spider mums, remove flower buds that have formed along the sides of each stem. This will encourage the plant to send more food to the terminal buds and thus produce larger blossoms.

Give each peony plant a light feeding: two tablespoons of 5-10-10 granules or two tablespoons of organic granules plus a tablespoon of bone meal.

Annual flowers

A final sowing of zinnias and a few other fast-growing annuals can be made during the first week of August. Cut back wax begonias, ageratum, vinca, torenia and petunias if they've gotten too leggy, then feed with liquid fertilizer to stimulate new blooms. Coleus plants can also be trimmed if they've gotten awkward-looking.

Pansies and other super-hardy annuals can still be started from seed for fall bloom.

Herbs

To start a collection of herbs to grow indoors during the winter, make divisions or take cuttings of woody plants and plant seeds of dwarf basil, dill 'Bouquet' and parsley. These can all grow outdoors in pots until next month, then come inside.

Vegetables

Continue watering and fertilizing established plants. Pick vegetables and melons as they ripen. Winter squash is ready to harvest when rind is hard and cannot be punctured with thumbnail. Pull out plants that have stopped producing, including bush beans, summer squash and early cucumber. If okra production has slowed, prune off the top third of each plant to force the development of side shoots.

When flowers begin to form on Jerusalem artichokes, cut off the top two feet or so. Removing the flowers in this manner allows the plants to direct more energy toward increasing tuber size. Still, the blooms are so pretty that you may want to sacrifice a bit of your harvest by allowing one or two plants to come into bloom. The sunny yellow flowers can be cut and placed in a vase or simply enjoyed in the garden as they grow.

August 1-15, set out tomato suckers that were rooted in July. Make a last planting of bush beans and carrots. You can even try a last round of cucumbers and summer squash during the first week.

Some gardeners plant pre-sprouted seeds of various green peas (snow, sugar snap or garden) which take 60 days or less to begin bearing. The pre-sprouting ensures they will come up fast even though the earth is hot. With luck, the vines will flower and bear before all the flying insects needed to pollinate them are dead and gone.

Sow seeds of many cool-weather vegetables, including mustard, kohlrabi, rape, rutabaga, Swiss chard, Chinese cabbage and beets.

Sow crimson clover, cowpeas or other green manure plants as a cover crop in areas of the garden that will remain unplanted until late next spring.

August 16-30, set out transplants of broccoli, Brussels sprouts, cauliflower, collards and celeriac. Continue planting mustard and rape, make a last planting of collard seeds and a first planting of spinach, kale and leaf lettuce.

Seedlings: Aug. 1-15, start Brussels sprouts and cabbage if not done in July. Also start Swiss chard and kale to set out in September. Leek seeds started now can be set in the garden later on and will be ready to eat in early spring. August 16-30, start leaf lettuce and kale.

Fruit

Prop up heavily laden branches of peaches, pears, apples, etc., to prevent breakage. Early pears are ready to pick when they separate from the branch as you tilt them gently upward.

Cut off the old canes of blackberries and raspberries that bore fruit earlier in the summer. Don't touch the newer canes that have never flowered. The new canes of everbearing varieties will soon begin to bloom and produce a fall crop while those of the one-crop varieties will produce next year's fruits. For ease of care and harvest next year, you may want to thin out the new canes of the once-a-year varieties to three or four per hill or a foot apart in rows. After pruning, weed thoroughly, feed lightly and renew the mulch.

Feed strawberries about mid-month.

Take time out to weed the blueberry patch and trim off diseased or dead branches. Remove bird netting that was put up earlier.

House plants

House plants can stay outside through the end of August. To turn summer annuals into household residents for the winter, take cuttings of coleus, impatiens, begonias and geraniums. They should root and be growing well by the first of October. Nasturtium seeds can be planted in pots to produce blooming house plants, though they will thrive only if grown in a cool but sunny windowsill (often impossible in this area).

Plant freesia bulbs in pots now for winter bloom.

Around the middle of the month, stop watering amaryllis bulbs. Put them, still in their pots, in a dark, dry location (basement or closet). Leave them there for at least a month before bringing them out into the light to start the blooming process. Some gardeners like to tip the pots over on their sides during this rest, but others feel that it doesn't make any difference.

An alternative method to dealing with amaryllis bulbs is to stop fertilizing them at the end of August but keep watering them regularly. Bring them inside to their normal location in September. The leaves may look tattered, may even die, but watering shouldn't cease. Bloom spikes should appear in January or February, and fertilization can be resumed after they've faded. Aficionados of this approach feel the bulbs produce more flowers than when subjected to the forced dormancy routine.

Notes

September

Kudzu vines flower rampantly in September, along with sweet autumn clematis and wild asters. The first dying leaves begin to flutter down and polkweed seeds turn from green to purple. Although the beginning of September may still seem like summer, temperatures usually fall by the end of the month, and cool-weather flowers and vegetables begin to perk up.

Soil test

September is the ideal month for taking soil samples to be tested by the Agricultural Extension Agency that serves your area. Carefully follow directions given by the agency. Label each sample with the type of plant to be grown in that area so testers can make appropriate recommendations. Keep a record of which soil sample is which so you can put test results to good use during the coming winter and spring months.

Lawns

Lawns of all kinds will probably need regular mowing all month.

Warm-season grasses should be fed early in September if it was not done last month. This is also the month to overseed these grasses with rye for winter color.

Feed fescue and bluegrass in mid-September with a synthetic or organic slow-release formula to support renewed growth as the weather cools. Re-seed bare areas or start new lawns. For best results, buy one of the newer turf fescues that has been bred specifically for your area. The seed may seem slightly more expensive than something like Kentucky 31, but the grass it produces should be much healthier and longer lasting. Prepare ground carefully and water attentively for good germination and growth.

Ground covers

Cut fading flowers from liriope plants unless you like the dark seeds that will form. Leaving the seeds on can also result in lots of baby plants sprouting up next spring in unexpected places, something which may — or may not — be desirable in your landscape.

Shrubs and trees

Surprisingly enough, the end of September is a good time of year to prune maple trees. There will be less bleeding of sap from cut limbs now than there would be from a late winter pruning. Overgrown crabapples also can be cut back.

Give buddleias a light trim by removing old blossoms and ungainly limbs at the start of the month. Feed afterward to induce more fall flowers.

Spend some September hours thinking about where to plant new trees or shrubs. Since leaves are still clinging to deciduous trees, you'll have a more accurate idea about sunny and shady areas if you look around now than if you wait until the trees are bare.

As you think, be absolutely realistic about the mature height and width of each tree and shrub. A willow, magnolia or blue spruce may look cute at five feet, but in 15 years its size can make for major problems.

A mistake new gardeners frequently make is to put a perfectly wonderful tree or shrub in the wrong place. Variegated privet, for instance, is never going to be beautiful if planted in a dark nook or cranny, yet a rhododendron absolutely requires a partially to fully shady spot for survival. Research the needs of plants before you buy.

Another common blunder is to plant tall, fast-growing shrubs under low windows. They will require an inordinate amount of pruning in years to come, something that could be avoided by seeking out shrubs that have a naturally low height at maturity.

Once a plan has been made, begin digging holes on cool days to save labor later.

Hedges

Evergreen hedges such as privet, Korean box, holly and photinia can be trimmed at the start of the month. There is just enough time left for some new growth to appear, cover the scars and harden before winter sets in.

Vines

Try to cut off and dispose of seeds as they begin to form on morning glory and cypress vines. Those allowed to mature and fall to earth will sprout next year and cause a weeding headache. You may want to try to gather seed sometime this month from some of your more unusual annual vines to save for planting next spring.

Roses

Roses revive in September. Repeat bloomers put out a new flush of blossoms and may continue flowering into December. For best results, fertilize these plants at the start of the month, water deeply, remove faded flowers and pay attention to disease control.

Summer bulbs

Lycoris (spider lily) usually sends up spikes of flowers this month. As they fade and the foliage appears, scratch some bulb fertilizer into the ground.

Spring bulbs

Bulbs usually arrive at local nurseries in September, even though it is too early to plant them. Buy now while selection is good, but store in a cool place (basement or refrigerator vegetable crisper) until late October or early November. Store in paper bags, not plastic, to forestall fungus problems. Also avoid storing tulips near apples; the gas given off by ripening apples may cause bulbs to rot.

Toward the end of the month, dig, divide and replant beds of lily-of-the-valley which may have become overcrowded.

Forced bulbs

Purchase paperwhite narcissus for winter bloom. Pot up a new batch of bulbs every couple of weeks. Store extra bulbs in a cool, dry place; the vegetable crisper of the refrigerator is ideal, as long as it never falls below 32° F.

Delphiniums

As experienced gardeners know, delphiniums do not love most of the Piedmont Plateau. One way to get around survival problems is to treat them as super-hardy annuals.

Start the seeds now, in a shaded seedbed or indoors under lights. Transplant them to a sunny spot in the garden during December (they'll be happy as clams thinking it's just a normal summer in Maine). Then fertilize the heck out of them and water regularly. They should begin blooming in the late spring.

Pull up and discard the plants as the last flowers begin to fade, then set out something different to provide flowers for summer and fall.

Perennial and biennial flowers

Remember to continue to water perennials to ensure their survival. Set out biennial transplants toward the end of the month as the weather cools. Also set out any perennial transplants grown from seed sown in July or purchased from a nursery.

Perennials that bloomed in spring or summer, including hosta, can be divided now and replanted.

New peonies can be set out toward the end of September if there has been a cold rain and the ground is not too hot. If weather is steamy, wait until October.

Plant peonies shallowly, so that root tops are just an inch under the surface of the soil. If plant is container grown and not yet dormant, trim off any broken or dead branches and cut back the whole plant so it is about eight inches tall. Peonies need only a half-day of sun in this climate and prefer fertile soil that has been enriched with bonemeal. They don't like to compete with tree roots, so try to place them away from the drip-line of tall trees; if this isn't possible, at least be sure to fertilize and water regularly.

Mid-sized chrysanthemum plants are available at nurseries this month. Smaller ones sold at the start of the month will continue to grow for six or eight weeks before blooming later in the fall. Larger ones, which usually go on sale in the middle of the month, are already in bloom and will brighten the garden immediately. For good growth, feed regularly and provide plenty of water after setting out. Check for aphids and spray with agricultural soap if necessary.

Annual flowers

Trim back leggy plants and continue to remove faded flowers to encourage more blooms.

Collect seed from non-hybrid annuals to plant next year.

Pansies can be set out right away if you've grown your own, or as soon as they are available at local nurseries. They are hearty eaters, so mix ample fertilizer plus some lime or wood ashes into soil before planting.

Set out ornamental cabbage and kale for winter color at the end of the month. Try to place these hardy plants in a spot that is readily visible from the house so you can look out and enjoy them throughout the winter. Don't worry if they don't have much color right now; as the weather cools, the new growth will take on brighter hues.

Depending on your local mini-climate, nurseries also may offer several interesting fall- and winter-blooming bedding plants now, including calendula, alyssum, snapdragon and certain strains of dianthus. If so, they can be set out right away. They will bloom until cold weather hits hard, and most of them will survive the winter to flower prolifically early next spring.

Herbs

Continue drying herbs for winter use, but taste them before you do this. Those that are currently in flower or have just finished may not be as full of flavor as you would wish.

If fresh fall dill is available, chop the leaves and freeze with water in ice cube trays. Snip off long stems of parsley with attached leaves and place in a bag or jar in the freezer. Take out desired amount later and then chop just before using. Chives can be chopped, frozen in a single layer on trays, then quickly placed in pre-chilled containers and returned to the freezer; this should prevent them from sticking together in an unmanageable lump.

If you'd like to give herbs as a Christmas, Hannukah, Ayyam-i-Ha or other mid-winter present, start now by potting up divisions, taking cuttings or planting seeds. Grow outdoors until the end of the month and then bring indoors to a cool but bright place.

Dig and divide large clumps of chives.

If you need more parsley, set out transplants now to provide winter picking in all but the coldest parts of the Piedmont Plateau. If you don't have any transplants, plant seeds instead. They will sprout in about 20 days, stay small during the winter and then produce lush growth in the spring.

Vegetables

Continue watering and fertilizing vegetables, especially those planted last month. Dig and divide beds of multiplier onions. Plant the small Egyptian onion sets that you gathered from the mother plants in June. Put out onion sets or plants anytime this month.

All sorts of other fall vegetables can go in right away, including transplants of leaf lettuce, Swiss chard, broccoli, Brussels sprouts, cauliflower and cabbage. After mid-month, pinch new blossoms off tomatoes, peppers and eggplants to help smaller fruits mature before cold weather.

Harvest peanuts when shells become hard. Sweet potatoes are typically harvested in early October, but some varieties may be ready now. Dig gently underneath plants to check on tuber size.

Weed the asparagus bed. Feed with commercial granules, organic formulas or an inch or two of finished compost plus a sprinkle of lime or wood ashes. Add a few inches of mulch if it's getting thin.

Dig up leeks planted last year which sent up flower stalks this past spring. The base of each leek will have split into several small bulbs, each of which can be broken off and replanted. They'll grow well for the rest of the fall and will be ready for harvesting and eating between mid-winter and early spring.

I find this method of leaving a few leeks in the garden each spring to grow over the summer and form new bulbs for fall planting is much easier than trying to start a crop from seed each year. If, however, you do want to grow them from seed, you might want to experiment with sowing them in late August or early September and transplanting them to the garden at the start of November.

They won't be ready for use during the winter but should be large enough to eat next spring. This method works for many Piedmont gardeners and has the advantage of not taking up any garden space during the summer.

Sow a hardy cover crop such as hairy vetch, crimson clover, winter rye or wheat on cleared spots in vegetable garden.

Sept. 1-15, plant leek seeds or bulblets from divided clumps, radishes, mustard and rape. Make a final sowing of leaf or semi-heading lettuce, bok choy, beets, arugula, corn salad, garden cress, kale, spinach and turnips.

Sept. 16-30, plant yet another round of radishes, plus more mustard and rape if necessary.

Fruit

Keep watering fall-bearing raspberries, figs, strawberries and other late fruits. Protect from birds if necessary, as mentioned in June notes.

Harvest apples as they mature; clean up fallen fruit to control insect and disease problems.

Dig and transplant runners from overgrown strawberry beds or set out newly purchased plants. Fertilize all strawberries with a slow-release substance such as compost, rotted manure or cottonseed meal.

Mow and rake under nut and persimmon trees so the fruits and nuts will be easier to find as they fall.

Continue tip-pruning fruit trees until the middle of the month.

House plants

House plants should be brought inside by mid-to-late September, even if days are still warm. Because indoor and outdoor temperatures are nearly identical for much of the month, the move is far less stressful for the plants now than it will be later when it's cool outside but furnace-heated indoors.

Begin preparing plants right away for the move indoors by trimming back leggy growth and checking carefully for insects. If you suspect beetles have crawled in through drainage holes, knock plants out of pot, take a look, crush and destroy insects and then replace plant in pot.

To foil insects, spray house plants twice with agricultural soap or pyrethins, once at the start of the month and again just before they're brought inside.

When soil in pot looks caked and stiff, loosen the top couple of inches, dump it out and replace with new potting soil. If fertilizer salts have formed a white crust on the soil or on the outside of clay pots, leach them out by applying so much water the liquid soaks completely through the soil and runs out the drainage holes in huge quantities, carrying dissolved salts with it. It may also be wise to scrub off the outside of clay pots.

There are a few exceptions to the move-it-inside-now rule: plants that need decreasing sunlight and cool weather to bloom should stay out until late October (or until the first frost is predicted). These plants include Christmas and Thanksgiving cactus, jade plant and some orchids.

If amaryllis bulbs weren't put aside last month, do it now unless you're following the alternate procedure mentioned in August's notes.

Notes

October

October is a wonderful month to be outdoors. The air is crisp, skies are blue for days on end and cool-weather crops grow vigorously. Leaves begin to change color, and many trees are at their peak during the last half of the month. October is a good time for major projects, such as building a brick wall, repairing raised bed edgings or erecting a gazebo.

The first frost may arrive at the end of October, but city yards and sheltered gardens usually escape damage until November, or even December in mild years. Write down the date of the first killing frost in your yard as a reference for future years and check with neighbors if you're new to the area. Toward the end of the month listen to weather forecasts each night and prepare to protect tender plants, such as tomatoes and impatiens, to prolong the harvest.

Compost

Compost is a word that should be a familiar part of every gardener's vocabulary. As leaves begin to fall in earnest, gather them up and save every single one. When mixed with other ingredients, like chopped weeds, garden thinnings, kitchen parings and even hair clippings, they will become valuable humus (the fancy name for decayed organic matter).

Making compost is beneficial to both our neighborhood and our planet since it is a non-polluting way of reducing garbage and producing free fertilizer/soil conditioner through intelligent recycling.

Finished compost (which is dark brown, crumbly and smells woodsy rather than rotten) is used as both a soil conditioner and a gentle fertilizer for all manner of growing things, including vegetables, flowers, shrubs, small trees and lawns. Finely sifted compost is an excellent addition to the mix used for growing transplants or house plants.

There are several ways to gather leaves and numerous methods of building compost piles. Rake up whole leaves and heap them in slow-rotting piles or use a mower or shredder to slice them into smaller pieces to rot faster. Use some right away, save other heaps to be mixed with clippings to make hot piles next spring and summer.

After reading more about composting at the public library or learning about it from the local Agricultural Extension Service, you'll be ready to choose among the three basic types of compost piles:

1. A fast-rotting pile of well-shredded layers of leaves and green vegetable matter plus manure (optional) and soil. The whole pile is built at one session, turned over and re-wetted every week or two, heats up in the middle once or twice and is ready to use in six weeks. It produces fast, excellent compost in which most weed seeds have been killed. But, and this is important, it takes plenty of work.

2. A slower-to-rot but easier-on-the-back pile that is built up over the course of several weeks or months as shredded leaves and other ingredients become available. When the pile is large enough it is turned and mixed just once, perhaps given an extra boost of manure, fresh grass clippings or other high-nitrogen material, and left to rot for several more months before use. The pile may heat up for a short time after the mixing. Although some weed seeds are killed because they germinate

and then smother, others may survive to sprout after the compost has been spread on the garden.

3. The long-term but exceedingly easy pile. Leaves and other matter may or may not be shredded. Everything is thrown on as available and rots slowly. The pile is never mixed or moved and may be built over some sort of partial support with an opening so that decayed material can be shoveled out from underneath without disturbing the top layers. Weed seeds are rarely killed in this pile, but it sure is simple.

4. It's also possible to evade the building of piles completely using either sheet composting or trench composting. The first requires that organic matter be spread over the surface of the garden, usually in late fall, and then tilled in.

Trench composters, on the other hand, begin by digging a long, deep furrow along one edge of the garden. Everything that can rot is thrown into the furrow until it is full. At that point, a second trench is dug next to the first. The soil from it is used to cover the material in the first one, then the second one is gradually filled with leaves, kitchen waste, etc. And, of course, a third trench is dug, and a fourth, and so on. Little by little, every section of the garden receives this treatment, which slowly but steadily enriches the soil with the passing months and years.

Lawns

Warm-season grasses usually begin to brown in October as dormancy sets in. It's not too late to overseed these grasses with annual rye for winter green, though you should finish the task before mid-month. Take into consideration the fact that overseeding is becoming more controversial these days because many horticulturalists feel the presence of actively growing rye weakens the dormant grasses.

Cool-season grasses are generally lush and need occasional mowing. Set blades a bit lower than in the summer to keep grass at about two inches high going into the winter. Feed immediately if not done in September. There's still time to reseed bare areas or start a new lawn, but try to finish planting by mid-month.

Shrubs and trees

Recent research has shown that fall feeding of shrubs and small trees helps them get through the winter in good shape. Evergreens retain leaves better after a fall feeding; deciduous plants have more intense fall colors and are stronger as they go into dormancy. The best time to feed them in the Piedmont

Plateau is during the last week of September or the first two weeks of October.

Use of a slow-release formula is essential so plants aren't spurred into new leaf production by excess nitrogen. A mulch of newly finished compost will work well, as will general organic fertilizers or special fall formulas. Acid-loving plants can be given a dose of cottonseed meal or an azalea/camellia formula.

If there aren't any plants with fall berries in your yard, browse at a nursery this month to see what's available. Some berried plants attract birds, while others are purely ornamental.

Container-grown or balled-and-burlapped shrubs and trees can be planted any time this month.

Vines

Bittersweet that is gathered before frost and dried should retain its decorative colors for several months. Gather seed to save from unusual annual vines early in the month, before they are withered by frost.

Roses

Repeat bloomers respond to the September feeding and cooler weather with stunningly beautiful flowers this month. Continue watering, spray only if necessary (insects aren't much of a problem now) but don't feed again.

Toward the end of the month stop removing faded blossoms. This allows hips (seed pods) to form and helps trigger winter dormancy.

Spring bulbs

Bulbs can be planted at the end of October. Choose a well-drained site that is not soggy during winter or spring rains. Prepare soil by spading or tilling a foot deep. Spread bulb fertilizer at bottom of hole or bed, cover with a thin layer of earth and then set bulbs into place at the recommended depth.

While setting out new bulbs, also feed bulbs planted in previous years by scratching bulb fertilizer into the topsoil, mulching with well-rotted manure or spreading out a layer of finished compost plus some bone meal. This fall feeding is the most important one to keep bulbs blooming from year to year. Water well to begin moving nutrients down into the soil.

Forced bulbs

Continue potting groups of paperwhite narcissus for winter

bloom. For indoor color in late winter, fill pots with forcing varieties of tulips, hyacinths, daffodils and other spring bulbs. Add one teaspoon of bulb fertilizer to the soil of each pot. Forced bulbs need cool temperatures, but a super-hard freeze could injure them. So, place pots in the corner of an un-heated basement where temperatures remain between 40° F and 50° F or bury them up to their rims in the ground and cover with a deep, insulating layer of leaves. Or, remove the bottom of a plastic foam cooler, place in a completely shaded spot, set planted pots inside, fill with dry leaves and then put the top on the cooler. Pots can even be stored in the refrigera-tor (not the freezer!).

Check pots weekly and water just enough to keep soil evenly moist but not soggy. After approximately fifteen weeks of cool-ing, they'll be ready to bloom in a cool but sunny window.

Summer bulbs

Caladium, canna, gladiolus, tuberous begonia and other ten-der bulbs can be lifted for storage any time after mid-month. Clip off any foliage, allow to air-dry for a couple of days and place in ventilated bags of dry peat moss or sawdust. Store in a cool but frost-free spot out of direct light.

Dahlias bloom beautifully in cool weather, so you'll probably want to wait to dig and store the tubers until after plants are killed back by a hard freeze.

To tell the truth, some summer bulbs, including dahlia, canna and gladiolus, will actually live through most Piedmont winters, but the digging and storing process allows you to dis-card diseased tubers and propagate new plants by breaking off extra tubers or bulblets before spring planting. It also ensures that they don't rot if the winter is especially rainy or freeze to death if Arctic air flows our way.

Perennial and biennial flowers

Most perennials, including peonies and iris, can be set out anytime this month. There's still time to dig, divide and re-plant crowded spring and summer-flowering perennials.

Some lantana varieties have proven themselves hardy in much of the Piedmont Plateau. If you decide to leave them in the ground, don't cut off any of the foliage. Let it die back nat-urally and form a natural mulch for the plant. Then trim off dead areas in late spring when new growth has begun to show.

Pots of chrysanthemums that are beginning to bloom can be bought and set out for a spot of instant color. Loosen root ball thoroughly before planting and water often.

October 1-15, seeds of lunaria (money plant) sown outdoors should sprout now, then bloom next spring.

Geraniums

Bring geraniums in for winter storage during the last half of the month unless they are growing in an extremely sheltered area where temperatures will remain above normal for another month or two.

Storage techniques work best with plants that were bought or grown from cuttings this past spring; older plants that were stored last winter may be too woody to resprout next spring.

The idea is to put the plants in a dark, dry, cool but frost-free spot and leave them alone (no water or food) until March. Some gardeners tie string around the main stem, pull the plant out of its pot and hang it from a basement beam. Others just put the whole pot, plant and all, into storage. Both techniques work just fine, so choose the one that suits you best.

It is also possible to keep a geranium or two in a sunny window and then take cuttings in January to produce a bevy of new plants for next year's garden. If you decide to do this, prune the plant heavily now; it will produce a number of new shoots that will be perfect for cutting after the first of the year.

Annual flowers

Marigolds, impatiens, zinnias and other tender annuals should probably be pulled up toward the end of the month before the first frost hits, making plants slimy and hard to handle. It's sad to pull up living flowers, so cheer yourself up by planting something new in their place.

Snapdragons can be considered exceptionally hardy annuals or medium tender perennials in our climate. Feed lightly and cut off faded flowers and seedpods now to induce a flush of blooms in November. They may even live over the winter some years and produce early spring flowers. Interestingly, young snapdragons for sale now at nurseries usually have a better winter survival rate than older ones that have already been in the garden for several months.

Continue to set out pansies plus ornamental kale and cabbage. Clip dead blossoms from pansies planted last month and fertilize to encourage continued flowering.

October 1-20, plant seeds of super-hardy annuals that need cold weather to trigger germination, including cornflower, larkspur, Shirly poppy, Foxy foxglove, California poppy and Virginia stock. These can also be planted in November,

December, January or even early February if you're not in the mood to do it now.

Herbs

Most heat-loving herbs have lost considerable flavor by October. Discontinue drying them for winter use. Chives and parsley, however, taste better than ever in cool weather, so use them lavishly. French cooks mince fresh chives and parsley together and encourage diners to spoon desired amounts onto fresh vegetables or baked potatoes. The flavors complement each other and parsley cuts the oniony aftertaste of chives.

Bay plants must be brought inside early this month to overwinter unless you have an especially protected area in which to keep them....maybe a southern wall of the house near the swimming pool.

At the end of the month either bring rosemary plants inside or rig some sort of protection if you live in the cooler portions of the Piedmont. Thanks to Jim Wilson, I have learned to mulch the whole rosemary area with rocks (the size of a fist, a loaf of bread or even larger) and grow them that way year 'round. The rocks reflect extra heat in summer and keep plants very dry, discouraging fungal diseases. In the winter they store daytime heat and release it at night, providing a few extra degrees of freeze protection. When chunks of old concrete rubble are mixed in with the rocks, rain will slowly leach calcium from them into the soil, nudging it toward the alkalinity that rosemary prefers.

Vegetables

Listen for frost warnings and be prepared to cover tomatoes, eggplants, peppers and other tender vegetables. The weather often warms up again after the first frost, so this protection may prolong the harvest by two weeks or more. Remove any small, new fruits that form in order to force the plant's energy into maturing the larger ones.

When it is impossible or impractical to keep plants protected any longer, pull up and add to the compost heap or consign those with diseased foliage to the garbage can. Till or spade soil in cleared areas to expose insects that are trying to overwinter. Then plant a hardy cover crop, do some sheet composting or mulch bare soil with shredded leaves, fresh manure or spoiled hay to minimize winter erosion and provide nutrients for next year.

Cool-season vegetables perk up in October and grow vigorously. Water during dry spells and feed as necessary. Keep an eye out for cabbage loopers and aphids, usually the two most troublesome pests in October. Use Bt on the loopers, insecticidal soap on the aphids.

Thin turnip and radish plantings to give each root enough room to develop.

During the first week of the month, thin carrots to desired spacing and then sprinkle an inch of compost or a half-and-half mix of peat moss and bagged manure over the top of the carrot bed to provide needed nutrients and protect root tops.

Harvest sweet potatoes early this month when the soil is relatively dry. Although they might grow longer, cold rains could cause splitting or rotting. Let tubers sit on the soil for a few hours, then bring inside and cure by placing in a humid, warm (80° F to 90° F) room for ten to fourteen days. Or a humid and cooler (65° to 75° F) place, such as a garage or garden shed, for three weeks. Store in a dry spot at 50° F to 60° F.

October 1-15, plant onion sets and garlic cloves. Also plant fast-maturing turnips such as Tokyo market and quick-growing radishes such as French breakfast and China rose. In all except the coldest autumns, the turnips and radishes will be ready for the table by Thanksgiving.

Plant a crop of spinach for overwintering. It will grow a little this fall, stay dormant over the winter and then start to grow vigorously in early spring.

October 16-30, continue planting onion sets. If you have a cold frame, cloche or can cover beds with double layers of floating row cover over hoops during extremely cold weather, you may want to experiment with planting seeds of lettuce, garden cress, radish or other salad ingredients for all-winter eating.

Orchard and fruit

Clean up under fruit trees, disposing of all fallen fruits to forestall many disease and insect problems next year. Mow if necessary under pecan and other nut trees.

Clean up the blueberry patch and prune broken or diseased limbs. Give bushes a fall feeding of cottonseed meal and thicken mulch by adding pine needles or shredded oak leaves.

Continue to dig and transplant rooted strawberry runners to new beds.

When harvest of everbearing bramble fruits such as Heritage raspberries is finished, cut the old canes back to four or five feet high and thin to a foot apart if crowded. These canes will produce an early crop next year before dying. Add more mulch if necessary.

Many Piedmont gardeners have successfully overwintered

banana plants outdoors in the last few years. They allow the plant to be killed back naturally by frost, then mulch the area thickly. The mulch is removed in mid-April and new sprouts appear in a few weeks. This works best if plants are growing near a house, stone patio or brick wall that moderates winter temperatures.

House plants

October is a tempting time to shop for new house plants since nurseries usually have a wide selection. Calla lilies make unusual but attractive guests and may bloom for months if the pot is kept in a water-filled saucer and placed in full sun.

Move house plants inside early in the month if not done in September. Plants that need decreasing light and temperature to bloom, such as jade plant and Christmas cactus, can stay outside until just before the first frost.

To trigger bloom formation (colored bract formation, to be accurate), poinsettia plants must have temperatures that stay between 60° F and 65° F plus a short day of eight to ten hours of light followed by a long night — a full fourteen to sixteen hours of darkness each night between October 1 and mid-December. This is extremely important so you must do whatever it takes: place plant in the sunny window of an unused room where lights are never turned on at night; keep the poinsettia with your other house plants but cover it at 6 p.m. with a cardboard box and don't remove it until 8 a.m. the next morning; place plant in a dark closet each evening and bring out again to a sunny spot every morning, etc. Continue watering but cut feeding in half during this time. Once color begins to appear, the regular darkness at night is no longer necessary.

If you haven't given amaryllis bulbs a dormant period, check the August notes and use the alternate procedure. If, on the other hand, you did put them into storage at least five weeks ago, it's time to bring out one or two.

Scoop out the top inch of dirt from amaryllis pot and replace it with good potting soil mixed with a teaspoon of bulb fertilizer, two teaspoons of guano or a tablespoon of bone meal. Water once with tepid water and place in warm, bright spot. Do not water again until new growth, usually the tip of a flower bud, shows. Don't be discouraged if this takes a long time, perhaps even six weeks (applying gentle bottom heat may help speed the process). When something finally pokes up, place in a sunny window and begin regular watering, but don't start fertilizing until after blooms have opened and faded.

Notes

November

If the first killing frost didn't come in October, it will almost assuredly arrive in November, often during the first week. A few tomatoes, eggplants, marigolds and other summer plants may still be alive, but only the cool-weather plants really relish shivery mornings and shorter days. Many sasanqua camellias are in full bloom and falling leaves drip down in a steady patter, providing fodder for the compost pile.

Lawns

Lawns need little attention this month, except for regular raking of fallen leaves and one or two mowings of cool-season grasses.

Shrubs and trees

November is prime planting month for shrubs and trees because cooler weather minimizes plant stress. Wait until December to buy and plant bare-rooted items.

General rules for planting are:

1. Be realistic about conditions at the planting site: space available, soil characteristics, amount of direct sun, etc.

2. Choose healthy stock from a trustworthy nursery or order from a reputable catalog. Keep receipts; many nurseries will replace a plant that dies in the first few months.

3. Prepare planting site carefully. Dig hole twice the size of the root ball. In clay soil use a spading fork to poke holes in the sides and bottom of the hole; this makes it easier for roots to penetrate as they grow. When amendments such as peat moss are recommended (as they usually are for azaleas, camellias and rhododendrons), mix them into the soil that has been dug from the hole. The consensus these days is that most shrubs and all trees adapt better over the long run if no special soil conditioners are added at planting time.

4. Loosen soil ball of container-grown plants to encourage roots to spread out. If roots are tightly coiled, use a knife or small hatchet to slice through the sides of the ball. This seems cruel but is absolutely vital.

5. Don't remove burlap from bagged-and-burlapped trees until they have been set into place. Then remove strings and either cut off top portions of the burlap or spread it out and leave it in the hole. Roots will grow through as it rots.

6. Fill the hole with soil. Be sure tree or shrub is exactly at the level at which it grew previously (look for soil line marks on trunk). Use extra soil to make a water-retention ring around the plant. Don't stomp soil into place; this can compact it and break off roots.

7. Water thoroughly. If plant is large, fill in a few shovelfuls of dirt, pour on a bucket of water and then go back to dirt again. Alternating the dirt and water will cause hidden air pockets to collapse and fill with soil. Water regularly during the next year, soaking roots thoroughly.

8. Wait until spring to fertilize when plants put out new growth. Some gardeners like to apply a dose of root stimulator at planting time.

9. Immediate pruning is not necessary, but do remove broken or diseased wood and cut out limbs that rub against each other.

10. Mulch ground under plants with shredded bark, pine nee-

dles, chopped leaves, etc.

Vines

Toward the end of the month, cut common hop vines back to within a few inches of ground level and mulch lightly.

Roses

Bushes may be loaded with lovely flowers, but don't be fooled into fertilizing them. Lush new growth is the last thing you want this time of year. Prepare for cold weather by continuing to allow rose hips to form. Tie up loose canes of climbing roses.

Spring bulbs

Plant spring-flowering bulbs at any time this month. If the autumn has been a warm one, wait until the last half of the month, when the soil will have cooled.

Fertilize beds of established bulbs if not done in October.

Forced bulbs

During the first half of the month, pot up a last round of spring bulbs for forcing. Also continue to plant paperwhite narcissus indoors for winter bloom.

Summer bulbs

Tender bulbs and tubers that could be killed by winter freezes should be lifted, dried and stored if not done last month. Lift dahlias as soon as the tops have been killed by frost and follow storage procedures mentioned in October.

Remove dead leaves from lilies, amaryllises and other hardy summer bulbs that stay in the ground for the winter.

Perennial and biennial flowers

New plants can be set out any time, though it's best to finish by mid-month. This is also a good season for digging and moving clumps of perennials from one spot to another.

Check for volunteer seedlings. Dig and move them to a new home or leave in place if not crowded.

Peonies can be divided when foliage dies. Dig, cut into segments with three to five eyes each, and replant so eyes are just one inch below soil. Water well to wash dirt tightly around roots.

Toward the end of the month, trim back dying top growth of perennials like Shasta daisies, blue salvia, hardy ageratum, sedum, Himalayan anemones, coneflowers and Stokesia. Also cut off chrysanthemum stems as the plants finish blooming. Leave the tight cluster of leaves that has formed near the base of plants intact; this is frost-hardy foliage that will overwinter and begin growing again in the spring. Cut daylilies back to about four inches.

Annual flowers

Super-hardy annuals like pansies and ornamental kale and cabbage can still be set out, though you may want to apply a root stimulator at planting time to be sure they grow well. Make sure they're put in a sunny spot.

Look for volunteer seedlings of hardy annuals like larkspur, Johnny-jump-up, and althea zebrina. Dig and move to a new home or leave in place if appropriate.

Seeds of hardy annuals mentioned in October can also be planted this month.

Herbs

Most perennial herbs become fully dormant this month, with the exception of tough items like chives and parsley.

Clumps of chives and mint can be potted up at the start of the month and left outdoors until after the first hard freeze. Then cut back dead leaves and bring indoors; they will re-sprout and can be cut for fresh use all winter.

Indoor herbs growing in pots appreciate good air circulation, so open a window when it's warm enough, use a small fan near plants occasionally or even set plants outdoors for a few hours on mild days.

Vegetables

If tender vegetables are still alive, protect them from frost on cool nights with row covering or a blanket. This protection may keep them going to mid-month, but eventually you should harvest the remaining fruits and pull up the plants.

Continue harvesting and eating cool-weather crops as they mature. Harvest kale by picking just a few mid-sized leaves from each plant; this will encourage continued production of new leaves all winter. Kale thrives in the Piedmont and rarely needs protection.

Carrots should be ready for the table this month but can be dug and eaten throughout the winter. A light mulch of shredded leaves or straw on carrots, turnips and other root vegetables will help protect against freezing. Allow foliage to stick up and live until killed back by super-cold nights. If the winter is mild, then leaves will stay green the whole time.

Radishes become pithy if left in the ground too long, so harvest as they mature. Consider leaving one or two in the ground to overwinter; next spring they'll flower and produce edible seed pods.

In parts of the Piedmont Plateau, gardeners manage to grow things like lettuce, Chinese cabbage, spinach and sorrel all winter with the protection of a row cover, cloche or a cold frame. As mentioned last month, you may want to experiment to determine how well this works in your own garden.

As summer crops are cleared out, many gardeners like to do deep tilling or plowing of the garden to prepare it for next year, figuring the soil is easier to work now than it will be in the middle of a wet winter or the start of a soggy spring.

November 1-15, set out leek transplants started from seed in August or September. Feed them afterward. Also feed any established beds of leeks and hill up soil around the bases to blanch the bottom halves of the roots.

Fruits

It's not too late to set out new strawberry plants or move rooted runners. Protect all strawberry beds by heaping a three- to four-inch mulch of pine needles or straw around the plants (don't actually cover them up). This will pack down slowly over the winter and keep fruits from touching the ground next year.

Protect bark of young fruit trees from winter sunscald by wrapping with tree tape or fabric or painting with white latex paint.

House plants

Begin cutting down on the amount of fertilizer given to house plants that either never bloom or that have already bloomed for the year; they will enter semi-dormancy as days become shorter. Plants that will flower during the winter, like hibiscus, bougainvillea, cyclamen, African violet, streptocarpus, and evergreen amaryllis still need normal amounts of fertilizer. So will nasturtiums, begonias and other outdoor annuals that you potted up for indoor enjoyment.

If jade trees, Christmas cactus or other plants are still outdoors, be very, very careful. One freeze is all it takes to kill them. Bring Christmas cactus inside as soon as flower buds form on the ends of the stem. Keep in a cool but well-lit room (high temperatures may cause buds to fall off).

Bring out a couple more of your dormant amaryllis bulbs,

following instructions in October's notes. If you don't have any, buy new bulbs at a nursery. Inexpensive bulbs are available at discount stores, but flowers on the more expensive bulbs are usually larger.

Continue the 14-hours-of-darkness routine for poinsettias. Also begin giving rex begonias (beefsteak, begonia, silver-leaf, etc.) and kalanchoes the same treatment. This should encourage them to produce flowers in December or January.

Clivia often flowers in November. The red seed pods that form afterward are attractive, but it's probably best to clip them off so the plant will put its energy into producing more flowers next year.

Humidity for healthy house plants

Indoor plants prefer high humidity, but the air in most houses gets drier and drier as the heating system begins to work steadily. To increase humidity, do one of the following.

1. Place house plants in pebble-filled bowls of water, making sure the bottom of the pot is above the level of the water. As water evaporates from the bowls it will increase the humidity.

2. Mist plants once or twice a day using a spray bottle filled with water. This is a controversial technique that many gardeners now believe doesn't really help at all, but there are plenty of green-thumbers who absolutely swear by it.

3. Run a humidifier near the plants, keeping it on for several hours each day. Ultrasonic humidifiers are especially nice because the mist they produce is cool and can be aimed directly at plants.

4. Attach an automatic humidifier to your furnace so that water will be added to the air whenever the furnace turns on.

Notes

December

December is a month of fierce winds that clear the last leaves from most deciduous trees. Night temperatures may occasionally fall to under 20°F, cold enough to freeze a bucket of water and injure gardenias. Plenty of rain, sometimes even sleet, can be expected. In spite of this, there are also a number of warmish days that gardeners can spend outdoors.

Compost is still a big job in December as leaves, weeds and frost-killed plants are added to the pile (see October notes).

If you forgot to have your soil tested, do it now (see September notes).

December is a good month to catch up on your garden journal if you've been negligent (see August notes).

Plant protection

Plant protection begins to be very important in December. Temperatures in the low teens are not unheard of during the last half of the month, and plants caught unprotected may be frozen back to ground level or killed altogether.

Mulch keeps soil warmer and thus protects roots, so mulch perennial flowers, roses, late vegetables and shrubs with a two- to four-inch layer of pine straw, shredded bark or chopped leaves.

Anti-transpirant sprays protect evergreen plants by cutting down on the amount of moisture lost from leaves. This is extremely important when the air is warm, but the soil is frozen and roots cannot pick up extra water. Gardenia, camellia, oleander and tea olive are on the list of shrubs that may benefit from being sprayed when a cold snap below 25°F is predicted.

Lawns

Little care is required this month, though it is important to rake up the last of the leaves. A few cool-season grasses may need one mowing.

Ground covers, ornamental grasses

Ornamental grasses don't need to be trimmed back unless an ice storm has rendered them particularly unattractive.

Holiday greenery

When cutting branches from hollies or other evergreens for indoor decoration, remember this is actually pruning. Cut wood at 45° angle above a bud so new growth appears where you want it. Outward-facing buds will produce outward-branching twigs and thus a wider shrub. Growth from inward-facing buds will help thicken the inner foliage of a sparsely branched shrub.

An anti-transpirant can also be sprayed on Christmas trees to keep them fresh longer indoors and should definitely be used on live Christmas trees before they are planted outside.

Shrubs and trees

Continue to plant shrubs and trees of all kinds, following directions in the November notes. Spray evergreen shrubs and trees with an anti-transpirant at planting time.

December is also a good time to dig and transplant shrubs

and small trees, including wild seedlings and old boxwood. Get as big a root ball as possible, and trim branches by a third after planting.

Bare-rooted items that were ordered from catalogs may arrive this month. Soak them in tepid water for a few hours before planting.

Vines

Give wisteria a good trim. Cut back by half or more all the long shoots that have formed in the last few months. After pruning, scatter superphosphate on the earth around the vines, using a half-pound for each inch of stem diameter.

This is a good time to prune English ivy and/or pull it off of house walls or trees. Ivy tendrils are not good for wooden shingles or for the mortar in brick walls. Vines that grow up into a tree may eventually cover too much of the foliage and cause the tree to die.

If ivy has already risen to absurd heights in a tree, the best approach is to cut through all of the vines, either right at ground level or a few feet up the trunk of the tree. A tough, sharp knife can be slid between the ivy and the bark, then pulled toward you to slice through the vine. Once this is done, the ivy high up in the tree will slowly die, look horribly unattractive for a few months and then, finally, shed all its leaves.

Roses

In mild years, some roses will bloom in December. As long as the plants have already formed a few hips, most of these last blooms can be cut for indoor enjoyment.

In the Piedmont, it is not really necessary to heap soil around the base of rose plants to protect them from winter cold the way Minnesotans do. Still, it's not a bad idea to thicken the mulch around the plant slightly since there may be a period of intense cold at the end of December or in January. You can also wrap burlap around an especially tender or vulnerable bush to make a cylinder, then fill it with shredded leaves.

Spring bulbs

Late bloomers can still be planted during the first week of the month, but bulbs that blossom in February (crocuses, snowdrops, etc.) may not flower this year if set out so late.

If you haven't already fed beds of established bulbs, do it now, using a good bulb fertilizer.

Don't worry if some spring bulbs have already pushed leaves

up; they will survive cold spells and bloom on time.

Forced bulbs

Continue watering pots of spring bulbs but don't move them into warmth or light yet.

Continue to plant paperwhite narcissus, either in soil or in containers filled with pebbles and water.

Summer bulbs

If dahlias bloomed right through the end of November, which occasionally happens, dig and store immediately (see October instructions).

Check bulbs that are already in storage to make sure they are still dry and rot-free. If there are signs of disease, cut off affected parts. Dust remainder with a fungicide, air-dry for two days and repack in new sawdust, peat moss or vermiculite.

Perennial and biennial flowers

Continue to cut back dying top growth of perennials, leaving untouched any crowns of newer foliage at the bases of these plants. Some perennials, like Asclepias (butterfly weed), die back completely, leaving no aboveground trace of themselves. This is perfectly normal, so don't worry about it, though you may want to mark a spot where the roots reside so you will not dig them up by mistake when you're messing around next spring. A brightly colored golf tee makes a good marker.

If temperatures fall below freezing for several days, check for frost-heaving (freezing soil may expand and thrust plants upward out of the ground). Set plants back in place once ground has thawed.

Annuals

In mild years, pansies and snapdragons bloom brightly in December and appreciate being fed at the start of the month. Ornamental kale and cabbage show more color as the weather cools. Feed all of these hardy annuals lightly at the start of the month to sustain continued growth.

Some Piedmont Plateau gardeners plant sweet peas in December for early spring bloom. I haven't had luck with this, but it's certainly worth experimenting with to see if you can do it.

Larkspur, cornflower, poppy and other hardy annual seeds can be sown now as mentioned in the notes for October.

Indoor seedlings: If you want to try raising begonias from seed, this is the month to start them because they are extremely slow-growing.

Herbs

Rosemary leaves are flavorful throughout the winter, and twigs can be snipped off for kitchen use at any time.

Continue to harvest parsley and chives and feed them lightly sometime during the month. If temperatures threaten to fall below 20°F, protect parsley with an overturned flowerpot, a deep mulch of straw or a floating row cover.

Vegetables

Vegetables protected by row covers or grown in cold frames may continue to produce well, so remember to harvest them. Jerusalem artichokes should be tasty by now, so begin digging and using the tubers.

Mulch carrots if not already done. Mound soil around leeks to blanch bottom half and fertilize lightly. Kale will appreciate a light feeding at the start of the month.

Turnips, cabbage, collards and most lettuces will not survive a sudden temperature drop below 15°F and must be either carefully protected or harvested when a super-cold night is expected. You may want to add a second layer of row coverings and also place a few old plastic milk jugs filled with water amid the vegetables underneath; these will serve as extra heat reservoirs and keep temperatures a smidgen warmer, perhaps just enough to prevent a total kill.

Take time to cut down the dead asparagus fronds and thoroughly weed the patch. Make sure you get the roots of perennial invaders like dandelions and plantain. When finished, sprinkle the ground with a light dose of superphosphate.

If soil is on the dry side, December is a good time to dig or double-dig intensive beds, especially those that will be used in February or March. Add plenty of organic matter while digging so that only a light raking will be needed at planting time. You can also turn under cover crops this month.

Indoor seedlings: December 16-30, start onion seeds.

House plants

Too much moisture can be as deadly as too little. Check plants carefully (get your fingers dirty!) before watering. As in November, only blooming plants need much fertilizer. Chinese hibiscus, in particular, needs warmth, lots of sun, water and fertilizer to sustain blooming.

Continue dark-at-night treatment for poinsettias until they have a good color, then bring out and treat normally. When rex begonias and kalanchoes have formed flower clusters, dark-at-night treatment may be stopped for them as well.

Remove decorative foil from the bottom of gift plants so water won't be held back and cause root-rot. Give Jerusalem cherries several hours of sun a day. Poinsettias do best with six hours of bright but indirect light.

Cyclamen needs a cool but bright spot and must be watered from the bottom. Place pot in bowl of tepid water for twenty minutes and let it soak up what is needed. African violets like this method of watering, too.

Gloxinias prefer bright but indirect light, warm night temperatures in the 60s, reasonably moist soil and moderate fertilizing. They must be allowed to go through a dormant period after bloom, so read about the cycle of care in a house plant book if you want to keep them for next year.

Notes

Notes